The Writer as Migrant

HA JIN

The Writer as *Migrant*

THE UNIVERSITY OF CHICAGO PRESS

CHICAGO & LONDON

The University of Chicago Press, Chicago 60637
The University of Chicago Press, Ltd., London
Published 2008
Paperback edition 2024
Printed in the United States of America

33 32 31 30 29 28 27 26 25 24   1 2 3 4 5

ISBN-13: 978-0-226-39988-1 (cloth)
ISBN-13: 978-0-226-83383-5 (paper)
ISBN-13: 978-0-226-39990-4 (e-book)
DOI: https://doi.org/10.7208/chicago/9780226399904.001.0001

Library of Congress Cataloging-in-Publication Data

Jin, Ha, 1956–
The writer as migrant / Ha Jin.
    p. cm. (The Rice University Campbell Lectures)
Includes bibliographical references and index.
ISBN-13: 978-0-226-39988-1 (cloth: alk. paper)
ISBN-10: 0-226-39988-5 (cloth: alk. paper)
1. Authorship—Philosophy. 2. Authors, Exiled. 3. Exiles' writings—
History and criticism. 4. Exiles in literature. 5. Emigration and
immigration in literature. 6. Language and culture—Philosophy.
7. Literature—History and criticism—Theory, etc. I. Title.
PS3560.16z46 2008
818'.54—dc22   2008012335

∞ This paper meets the requirements of ANSI/NISO z39.48-1992
(Permanence of Paper).

To Allen Grossman

Contents

Preface

Sometimes it is difficult to differentiate an exile from an immigrant. Nabokov was both an immigrant and an exile. But to the great novelist himself, such a distinction was unnecessary, as he often maintained that the writer's nationality was "of secondary importance" and the writer's art was "his real passport." In the following chapters, my choice of the word "migrant" is meant to be as inclusive as possible— it encompasses all kinds of people who move, or are forced to move, from one country to another, such as exiles, emigrants, immigrants, and refugees. By placing the writer in the context of human migrations, we can investigate some of the metaphysical aspects of a "migrant writer's" life and work.

I make references to many works of literature because I believe the usefulness and beauty of literature lies in its capacity to illuminate life. In addition, I focus on certain important works—texts that may provide familiar ground for discussion. I will speak at length about some exiled writers, not because I view myself only as an exile—I am also an immigrant—but mainly because the most significant literature dealing with human migration has been written on the experience of exile. By contrast, immigration is a minor theme, primarily American. Therefore, a major challenge for writers of the immigrant experience is how to treat this subject in response to the greater literary traditions.

My observations are merely that—my observations. Every individual has his particular circumstances, and every writer has his own way of surviving and practicing his art. Yet I hope my work here can shed some light on the existence of the writer as migrant. That is the purpose of this book.

The Writer as Migrant

The Spokesman and the Tribe

At the outset of his career, a writer often wrestles with the Aristotelian questions—to whom, as whom, and in whose interest does he write? His answers to those questions will shape his vision and help determine his subject matter and even his style of writing. Among the three questions, "as whom does he write" is the most troublesome one, because it involves the writer's sense of identity and tradition, both of which, though often not a matter of choice, may be subject to change.

My initial answers to those questions were quite simple. In the preface to *Between Silences,* my first book of poems, I wrote, "As a fortunate one I speak for those unfortunate people who suffered, endured or perished at the bottom of life and who created the history and at the same time were fooled or ruined by it." I viewed myself as a Chinese writer who would write in English on behalf of the downtrodden

Chinese. I was unaware of the complexity and infeasibility of the position I had adopted, especially for a person in my situation. Indeed, too much sincerity is a dangerous thing. It can overheat one's brain.

In general, writers from less-developed countries are apt to define themselves in terms of their social roles, partly because of the guilt they feel for emigrating to the materially privileged West and partly because of the education they received in their native lands, where the collective is usually held above the individual. In fact, the word "individualism" still has a negative ring in Chinese. When I began to write, I longed to return to China, and I saw my stay in the United States as a sojourn, so it felt almost natural for me to claim to be something of a spokesman for the unfortunate Chinese. Little did I know that such a claim could be so groundless. At any moment, a country can take a writer to task and even accuse him of misdeeds, betrayal, or other crimes against his people. Even the people he tries to serve can question him, "Who gave you the right to speak for us?" Some may even pose a challenge: "If you have not suffered together with us, you've just appropriated our miseries for your personal gain. You sell your country and your people abroad."

Few of those questioning the writer will heed the truism that Homer didn't have to go to Troy with the Greek warriors to sing of their deeds. But then, Homer is a great poet. Who are we? As aspiring writers, we at times cannot help but wonder about the justification for our writing endeavors. Can our talent alone be our justification as tribal spokespersons? Logically speaking, talent alone should be sufficient, since most collective experiences and personal stories have no lasting significance unless they are transformed and preserved in art. But the world operates in its own way, as if designed to frustrate and smother talent.

The best qualification for claiming spokesmanship that a writer can have is to be an established voice in his native country—that is, before arriving abroad, to already have an audience at home. From this position, he can resume writing abroad, though he may be speaking to different people and about different things. This is a fortunate endowment, but, like most endowments, it cannot last forever. Such a writer is like a literary ambassador of limited tenure who will be replaced by another in time.

It stands to reason that many important writers in exile regarded themselves as spokesmen of their native countries, because this approach is an expedient way to resume their writing roles. The best examples of this are the Russian novelist Alexander Solzhenitsyn and the Chinese author Lin Yutang, both of whom were exiles and viewed themselves as spokesmen of their countries, their visions shaped by nostalgia and by their efforts to rejoin their peoples after many years in the United States.

Solzhenitsyn was stripped of his Soviet citizenship for the false charge of treason. In December 1973, a Parisian publisher had brought out the first volume of *The Gulag Archipelago,* and he was expelled from Russia in February 1974. Although a man of strong self-assurance and moral conviction, he was staggered by the expulsion, unable to imagine living elsewhere or writing for a different audience. He told a Spanish interviewer, "I never intended to become a Western writer. . . . I came to the West against my will. I write only for my homeland." Also, to a Swiss reporter, he lamented, "I do not live in Switzerland. . . . I live in Russia. All my interests, all the things I care about, are in Russia."[1]

After two years in Europe, Solzhenitsyn and his family came to the United States in the summer of 1976 and secluded themselves in the outskirts of Cavendish, a village in the Black River Valley of Vermont. It was said that Solzhenitsyn loved the New England state's cold climate, crisp air, and natural forests, all of which reminded him of Russia.[2]

Last summer, I happened to take a trip to Vermont, and, while on my way back to Massachusetts, I drove to Cavendish to look at Solzhenitsyn's estate. To my surprise, the fifty-acre property, surrounded by a steel fence, was still inhabited by some members of his family. The iron gate was forbidding, complete with an intercom and electronic surveillance; nearby a tree bore a sign: "Private Property. No Trespassing." The road to his estate and the driveway inside the thickly wooded acres were both unpaved. His two-story wood house on a hill looked weather beaten, and around it nature appeared to have run its own course. A burbling brook flowed through a deep gully at the foot of the hill, making the place easy to defend from a military point of view—we know that the Solzhenitsyns occasionally received death threats even in Cavendish.[3] Everything beyond the steel fence seemed to suggest that the inhabitants had not intended to live here permanently, had been extremely concerned about their safety, and had deliberately isolated themselves from the public and their neighbors. On the other hand, a middle-aged woman at a grocery store in Cavendish gave me clear directions to the writer's home, fondly calling him "Alexander." My impression of his homestead was congruous with Solzhenitsyn's statement that he always planned to return to his native land.

He and his wife and their three sons lived at this place for eighteen years, until he was finally able to return to Russia, in March 1994—his Russian citizenship restored, the charge of treason dropped, and his books at last published in Russia. It was at this place where he worked twelve or fourteen hours a day, from 8 a.m. to 10 p.m., seven days a week, and wrote many of his books, mainly his magnum opus, *The Red Wheel* series.[4] Although he claimed, "I write only for my homeland," Solzhenitsyn for many years could not speak to the Russian people directly despite writing in his mother tongue. He could speak, through translation, only to a Western audience. All the same, he set himself the task of exposing the underside of the Soviet history, bearing witness to its destruction of humanity, and preserving the memories of the Russians who had no voice. This perspective made his later works more historical than literary: we can see that the books he wrote in Vermont are less literary than the novels he had written before his exile. In other words, by comparison, his early fiction, especially *One Day in the Life of Ivan Denisovich, The First Circle,* and *Cancer Ward,* is literature par excellence. Some people may think that these novels written in the realistic tradition are old fashioned, clumsy, tedious, and overpopulated, but each of them has a fictional autonomy that resists the passage of time. They will last. In contrast, his later books do not have a firm artistic order, and their relevance might fall to the erosion of historical change.

Before setting out for Russia in March 1994, Solzhenitsyn went into the Village of Cavendish, which he had rarely visited, and bade farewell to over two hundred villagers at a meeting. He said with gratitude, "Exile is always difficult, and yet I could not imagine a better place to live and wait and wait and wait for my return home than Cavendish, Vermont."[5] Obviously, to him, his eighteen years in the United States was just a long wait, during which, with his pen, he fought the Soviet regime and played a catalytic part in bringing it down.

Nevertheless, he was acutely aware that the new Russia differed greatly from the Russia he had left behind — the country had gone through Gorbachev's perestroika and was open to the influence of Western democracy and to the inroads made by capitalism. Although his literary books were well received in his homeland, his return was cautious and hesitant. It took almost two years for him to uproot himself from Vermont after Boris Yeltsin invited him to "work for the Russian people from within Russia and not from a foreign land." He felt he was going home to die and might not live for long once he was back in Russia.[6] For all that, his return was no less heroic and miraculous, considering that in literary history few banished giants succeeded in setting foot on their native soil again. In every way, his return is Odyssean.

Still, unlike Odysseus who restored his household and regained the kingship of his city-state, Solzhenitsyn had a rough time in his homeland. His patriotic views, mingled with Orthodox Christianity, fell on deaf ears, as his political books — *Russia in Collapse* (1998) and *Two Hundred Years Together* (2001) — were coldly received, and he was considered a has-been, out of touch with Russian realty. His TV talk show was cancelled due to low ratings. Solzhenitsyn, once a powerful spokesman in the West for the oppressed Russians and a impassioned critic of the Soviet regime, seemed to be losing his voice and unable to play any significant role in Russian society, like a retired diplomat whose career and service had taken place elsewhere. But Solzhenitsyn is Solzhenitsyn, as a genius is genius. In late January 2006, the state television broadcast a ten-part series adapted from his novel *The First Circle*. The show became one of the most watched programs on Russian television. Solzhenitsyn, now eighty-seven, wrote the screenplay and even narrated some long passages. It was said that he had turned tearful when he saw the edited version of the show.[7]

A decade after Solzhenitsyn moved back to his homeland, we can say that he had at last returned to Russia, finally having gotten the acceptance of his people—though we should also bear in mind that this return was possible mainly through literature. Granted, it is the political situation in today's Russia that allows for his literary works to participate in reshaping the nation's identity and cultural heritage, but, had he not written significant literature, Solzhenitsyn might never have found access to the Russians' hearts again. Together with *The First Circle*, other adaptations of Soviet era masterpieces were also televised, such as *The Master and Margarita*, *The Golden Calf*, and *Doctor Zhivago*, illustrating that, to achieve a return to favor with the Russian people, an author's physical presence on Russian soil was no longer a prerequisite. Even if Solzhenitsyn had not been back in person, his literary works would have found ways to return to his people.

Heroic and triumphant as Solzhenitsyn's return was, let us not neglect his frustration and torment during his years of exile. On June 24, 1985, inside the courthouse in Rutland, Vermont, a town twenty miles north of Cavendish, court officials and three rows of reporters and photographers were waiting for Alexander Solzhenitsyn to appear and take the oath of U.S. citizenship. His wife, Natalya Solzhenitsyn, and his son Yermonlay were there, and everyone was waiting—but the writer never showed up.

Mrs. Solzhenitsyn explained that her husband was "not feeling well," but a friend of the family revealed that he was, in fact, fine. A month before, the family had applied for U.S. citizenship, and a special ceremony was arranged for them for June 24. On that day, Mrs. Solzhenitsyn received her certificate of citizenship alone, and she told the reporters she would apply for naturalization for her three sons now that she had become a citizen.[8]

Obviously, Solzhenitsyn changed his mind at the last minute and could not go through with the ceremony. Why then had he applied for the citizenship in the first place? Joseph Pearce, who apparently knew the Solzhenitsyns well, offered the following explanation:

> Years later the mystery surrounding his non-appearance was explained by Alya. Throughout the years of exile, her husband "never wanted to, and did not, become a US citizen, since he could not imagine himself to be a citizen of any country except Russia (not the USSR!)." During the early eighties, at the height of the Afghan war and at a time of failing hopes for short-term change in the USSR, Solzhenitsyn did in fact experience a moment of some doubt, but ultimately he decided to "remain stateless—right up until Russia's liberation from communism, an event for which he had always hoped."[9]

This explanation sounds reasonable. Nonetheless, it cannot explain away the fact that Solzhenitsyn almost became a U.S. citizen and had for some time lost "the animal indifference" and "the writerly assuredness" he eulogized in his fiction.[10] He must have been sick of the long wait, sick of being a refugee without a country, and sick of the role of a spokesman for a country that could not hear him and would pay no heed to his service. Above all, as a father and a husband, he must have sought the best way for his family to live. Like any individual, he was entitled to have self-doubt and to give up his native land if need be. Yet for a writer of his stature and social role, Solzhenitsyn could not have afforded to become a citizen of another country. If he were a U.S. citizen, his return to Russia would have been much more complicated and frustrating, because his opponents, even some ordinary Russians, would have treated him as an American and raised doubts about his allegiance.[11] Such a move would have undercut his credibility when he kept propounding the necessity of nationhood, a core value in his thought. Fortunately, he was coolheaded enough to restrain himself from attending the naturalization ceremony.

This episode in Solzhenitsyn's life shows that despite the writer's careful construction of his relationship with his tribe, his role remains susceptible to change—any accidental, sometimes necessary, step might easily undermine the construction and force it to drastic revision. By writing about Solzhenitsyn's attempted naturalization, I do not intend just to point out the folly this great man almost fell into. What I mean is to illustrate the fragility of his identity as a spokesman for his people.

In fact, I am always moved by Solzhenitsyn's bravery and his acceptance of isolation as the condition of his work. "All my life consists of only one thing—work," he once said. The village of Cavendish didn't even have a doctor at the time, according to his biographer D. M. Thomas,[12] and, because of sciatica, the aging Solzhenitsyn would stand at a lectern when writing. What made him so tenacious, I believe, was not only his dedication to work but also his Christian faith, which had inculcated in him a sense of continuity beyond this life. The belief in the afterlife can enable one to live this life fearlessly. At an interview before departing for Russia, Solzhenitsyn was asked if he feared death, and he replied with obvious pleasure on his face: "Absolutely not! It will just be a peaceful transition. As a Christian, I believe there is life after death, and so I understand that this is not the end of life. The soul has a continuation, the soul lives on. Death is only a stage, some would even say a liberation. In any case, I have no fear of death." In another context he said, "The goal of Man's existence is not happiness but spiritual growth."[13] That may account for the spiritual strength with which he completed his work in exile.

His words remind me of my meeting with a group of Chinese poets in River Falls, Wisconsin, in the summer of 2001. One of them was my former schoolmate. He greatly admired the small midwestern town because its climate and landscape brought to mind the northeast of China where we were both from. I asked him, "If possible, would you mind living in this town alone so that you can concentrate on writing poetry?" He answered, "I need a friend at least." That was a typical Chinese answer. The Chinese mind does not rely on a power beyond humanity for spiritual sustenance. This explains why very few Chinese exiles in North America have lived in isolation and why most of them have been city dwellers. Gregariousness is only a surface characteristic, and deep down it is the absence of the religious belief that produces a different outlook on life.

The writer Lin Yutang (1895–1976) discusses the Chinese ideal of life at length in his book *My Country and My People* (1935).[14] He points out that to the Chinese the essence of the ideal life is the enjoyment of this life. In the absence of a belief in an afterlife, the Chinese hold dearly on to this life and try their hardest to make the best of it. As a result, most Chinese fear death and the isolation that leads to loneliness. Their ideal of life, according to Lin Yutang, is "brilliantly simple" and is a "concentration on earthly happiness."[15] Confucius, the man who has influenced Chinese culture more than anyone else, once replied when asked about death, "I don't know enough about life, how can I know about death?" It is the deliberate focus on this life that makes the Chinese afraid of missing out on the joy this life offers and that makes them believe the best death is inferior to the worst life—a theme, the novelist Yu Hua dramatized eloquently in his novel *To Live* (1993).

Not as fortunate as Solzhenitsyn, the exiled Lin Yutang never managed to return to his native land. He too refused to become a U.S. citizen, though he lived in the United States for three decades.[16] Lin Yutang, a man of encyclopedic erudition, sharp wit, and practical vision, viewed himself as a cultural ambassador. Before he earned his M.A. from Harvard (1922) and his Ph.D. from Leipzig University (1923), he had been known as a rising scholar in Chinese lexicography in China and had taught at Tsinghua University. His life exemplifies how the writer's role, whether as a spokesman or a "renegade" of the tribe, can be shaped, or misshaped, by national and international politics. His first English book, *My Country and My People* (1935), was written when he was still in China. He had been encouraged by his friend Pearl Buck, who also helped him with its publication. The book became a bestseller in the United States. A year later, in 1936, at the age of forty-one, Lin Yutang emigrated to America in order to devote himself to writing in English. When he was working on his most popular book, *The Importance of Living,* which would come out in late 1937, the Marco Polo Bridge

Incident occurred—and the Sino-Japanese War broke out. To support his motherland's struggle, Lin Yutang began to publish articles in the *New York Times,* the *New Republic, Time,* the *Nation,* and the *Atlantic* condemning the Japanese scheme to annex China and persuading the American people to support the Chinese cause. He even drastically revised the last chapter of *My Country and My People* before it went through its thirteenth printing, to make it more suitable for the united Chinese efforts to resist the Japanese invasion.

At the time, few Chinese officials in the United States had access to the public media, so Lin Yutang literally became a spokesman for China. His public role was acknowledged by the fact that, during his half a year's visit to China in 1944, President Chiang Kai-shek and Madame Chiang received him no fewer than six times.[17] The Nationalist government not only appreciated his propaganda writings, which had helped China gain the U.S. public support, but also liked his staunchly anti-Communist views.

It would have been foolish and selfish for a writer like Lin Yutang to remain detached while his motherland was burning. However, his view of himself as a cultural ambassador more or less determined the nature and even the quality of his writings. He admitted, "My advantage is to be able to speak about Chinese culture to foreigners while I can speak about foreign cultures to the Chinese."[18] During his lifetime, he published over sixty books; in English alone, he published forty titles, among which, seven are novels and the rest are nonfiction. The nonfiction list includes long and short personal essays; biographies of ancient Chinese figures; translations of ancient Chinese texts, such as Laotsu and Confucius; a volume of Chinese art theories; a history of the Chinese press; a bibliography of the Chinese masterpiece *Dream of the Red Chamber*; a political treatise; and public lectures. Obviously, he was a man of many facets, but his energy was diffused and his writing career was actually in decline after the late 1940s, when he was in his fifties and thought of returning to China. But that return would be out of the question as a result of the Communists' takeover in 1949.

Lin Yutang was an accomplished literary scholar and understood the logic and nature of literature. In the prologue to his first English book, he writes:

> the only way of looking at China, and of looking at any foreign nation, [is] by searching, not for the exotic but for the common human values, by penetrating beneath the superficial quaintness of manners and looking for real courtesy, by seeing beneath the strange women's costumes and looking for real womanhood and motherhood, by observing the boy's naughtiness and the girls' daydreams and the ring of children's laughter and the patter of children's feet and the weeping of women and the sorrows of men—they are all alike, and only through the sorrows of men and the weeping of women can we truly understand a nation. The differences are only in the forms of social behavior. This is the basis of all sound international criticism.[19]

Here, he argues for human similarity as the guiding principle of writing, a principle he adhered to in *My Country and My People*. Even today, many of the views and insights expressed in this book are still relevant and refreshing. To my mind, Pearl Buck's assessment of the book is still sound: "It is, I think, the truest, the most profound, the most complete, the most important book yet written about China."[20]

However, Lin Yutang deviated from the principle of similarity as he continued to write about China. Such negligence on his part had something to do with his vision of himself as a cultural interpreter of his nation for a Western audience. He was not satisfied with his remarkable achievement in his English essays and understood the hierarchy of literature, as he once wrote, "My ambition is that all my novels will last."[21] On the one hand, he knew that literature had its hierarchical order in which the personal essay, as a minor genre, remains at the bottom; on the other, he did not concentrate on fiction writing at all, especially in his later years when he often wrote a book a year without a clear literary purpose except for financial need. Among his novels, he was most proud of *Moment in Peking* (1939), a mammoth novel he wrote in one year, modeled after the style of *Dream of the Red Chamber*. Like the fate of his other novels except *Chinatown Family,* this book has long been out of print in English, but it's still read by the Chinese in translation, especially by readers in the Chinese diaspora. Ambitious and vast in design though the novel is, it is regarded as a minor work and has some inherent weaknesses. The most salient one is that the novelist had no eye for details, which prevented him from becoming a major fiction writer. Indeed, the novel offers a good deal of details of jewelry, clothes, furniture, gardens, and foods, but they feel like they were prompted by the author's reading of other books, not obtained from the author's own observations or imagination. In other words, they are bookish and derivative details, which do not reveal the characters' psychology or the quality of their daily life. As a result, the prose tends to remain on the surface of things and does not have enough of the texture that provides material sensation.

There are two other weaknesses that must have stemmed from Lin Yutang's vision of himself as a cultural spokesman of China. First, the narrator tries too blatantly to present Chinese culture to a Western audience. There are passages that read like miniessays about Chinese women's education, Chinese medicine, and Chinese belief in the balance of the Five Elements in making marriages.[22] These passages are not blended into the dramatic context, block the flow of the narration, and result in prose that feels crude and unfinished. Such crudeness is not merely a technical blunder. It reveals the novelist's inadequate vision. Just as a creative writer should aspire to be not a broker but a creator of culture, a great novel does not only present a culture but also makes culture; such a work does not only bring news of the world but also evokes the reader's empathy and reminds him of his own existential condition. If a novel by which the ambitious author will stand or fall, he should imagine what kind of cultural order the book may enter into should it succeed. Lin Yutang obviously did not entertain such a vision and indulged himself too much in explaining China. Throughout *Moment in Peking,* the narrative reveals that the book was written only for a Western audience.

The other weakness related to his "spokesmanship" is a benign presentation of the life of modern China, a period when the country was battered by wars and upheavals and when people's daily life was precarious and often disrupted. Among the oversized cast of eighty-odd characters, there is not a single evil person, which cannot be true to life. Granted, the author believed in Confucianism and the goodness of man, but such a sweetened narrative tends to soften the story to the genre of popular romance.

The translation of *Moment in Peking* is still read by Chinese readers mainly because it attempts to portray a panorama of modern China through the saga of three families. For a similar reason, Lin Yutang's *Chinatown Family,* a novel about the American immigrant experience, has just been brought back into print by Rutgers University Press. This novel is not an essential piece of fiction in his corpus, but, because it is about the American experience, it is still read in the United States. Among all his books written in English, only this novel and his masterpiece of nonfiction *The Importance of Living* remain in print in English. This fact indicates that often it is not the language but the subject matter and the content that determine the life of a book.

In his seventies, Lin Yutang spent five years (1967–72) compiling a large dictionary, the *Chinese-English Dictionary of Modern Usage,* which he believed was the pinnacle of his literary career.[23] Interestingly, Solzhenitsyn also aspired to write a wordbook with an eye to preserving the purity of the Russian language that was violated by the Communist revolution and threatened by Western linguistic and cultural influences, and, in the early 1990s, he began to contribute a glossary to the Soviet Review *Russian Speech.*[24] Like most writers in exile, both Solzhenitsyn and Lin Yutang were obsessed with language, but Lin differed from Solzhenitsyn in intention—he attempted to serve as a linguistic bridge between English and Chinese. Initially, he embarked on his project with a mind to supersede the two Chinese-English dictionaries already in use ("the Mathews" and "the Giles"), which he thought could no longer meet modern readers' needs. Such a purpose was easily achieved when Lin Yutang's dictionary was brought out in 1972. However, six years later, Beijing Foreign Languages Institute published

A Chinese-English Dictionary (1978), which is not only more updated than Lin's dictionary but also more handy to use. The compilation of this official dictionary was ordered by Mao Zedong and attended to by Zhou Enlai; an editorial staff of over fifty people, Chinese and non-Chinese, spent eight years working on it. Ever since its publication, it has remained the standard Chinese-English dictionary and has been revised and updated regularly. Lin Yutang had a staff of three for his lexicographic project. It stands to reason that the dictionary by Beijing Foreign Languages Institute easily dislodged the position occupied briefly by Lin Yutang's dictionary.

In fact, in recent decades, reference books have been the forte of publishers in mainland China, where labor is cheap and where it is easy to gather collective efforts for a project that requires minimum creativity. For instance, the editorial staff of *A Great Chinese Dictionary* (1990), compiled by Wang Tongyi, was larger than two hundred people, full-time and part-time. It was a mistake for Lin Yutang to take on his dictionary project in the first place, and it was short-sighted for him to claim that it was the peak of his literary career, never mind that he might have had no inkling of what he was competing against in mainland China. An exiled writer must avoid pitting his individual effort against any collective effort, because his principal asset is his creative talent and energy, which should be used primarily for creative work—great literature has never been produced by collectives.

Unlike Solzhenitsyn who secluded himself and did not travel unless he had to, Lin Yutang, despite having New York City as his base, led a colorful, somewhat peripatetic life. He traveled through Europe frequently and was fond of the climate and lifestyle of southern France. In the mid-1940s he spent all his fortune, $120,000 in total, inventing the first portable Chinese typewriter. He did succeed in making such a machine, but owing to the Civil War in China, no manufacturer was willing to produce it; and the model typewriter was later junked. Consequently, the invention, potentially revolutionary and lucrative, bankrupted him. In 1949, he worked for the United Nations as a senior official in charge of arts and literature, but soon quit to write full-time. In 1954, he moved to Singapore to take the office of the founding principal of Nanyang University, but he resigned half a year later, having been sabotaged by the Communists. Throughout those years, he longed to go home, but this was impossible because of his anti-Communist stance. He often went to Hong Kong in his later years and stood atop a hill, gazing at his homeland beyond the border. The rivers and mountains were in view, but he could not return.

When Lin Yutang went to Taiwan to live in 1966, Chiang Kai-shek offered to have a house built for him as an expression of the Nationalist government's gratitude for his service, as if the writer were an official who had finally come home from a long stint abroad. Lin Yutang himself designed the house with the help of a noted architect. The house, white and topped with blue tiles, was exquisite, with a garden and a fish pond, constructed in a combination of the Chinese and the Spanish styles. Lin Yutang loved his house and seemed at home living there, though in reality it had been built with public funds. Since his death in 1976, the house has been a museum of his life and work.

Although not as fortunate as Solzhenitsyn and never physically present in his homeland again, Lin Yutang did return to mainland China through his literature. In 1987, the translation of *Moment in Peking* was finally published in China. Following the publication of this book, there appeared books on him and his literary accomplishments, though criticism of this kind is full of revolutionary clichés and patriotic platitudes. His collected works, in thirty volumes, were published in 1994. To date, millions of copies of his books have been printed in China, and he has become one of the most popular authors. There have been two competing TV series adapted from *Moment in Peking,* one made by Taiwan and the other by the mainland. The people of his hometown, Zhangzhou, Fujian Province, even built a museum dedicated to him with the help of the funds donated by his overseas fans. Yet beneath all the publicity, again we can see that it was his literary writings that met some cultural need of the newly opening China and thus paved the way for his return. Only through literature is a genuine return possible for the exiled writer.

In truth, other than slaking the writer's nostalgia, the writer's physical return to his native land has little meaning. The pages of literary history are studded with the names of exiled titans whose works, despite the authors' inability to go back to their native lands in person, were eventually embraced by their peoples. Dante, who accepted exile as the state of his historical being, never returned to Florence—and even his ashes were not allowed to return in spite of the repeated efforts made by some of his fellow citizens to have him back—but time and Italy have crowned him with poetic laurels. Joyce, who made exile the fundamental condition for his writing as if separation from Ireland was also an act of creation, was buried in Zurich, but his works have brought pride to the Irish and revolutionized modern fiction. The Chinese writer Eileen Chang died in Los Angeles in complete obscurity (in 1995), and for decades, her writings were unknown to Chinese readers, but her works of fiction are read widely as modern classics now. Only literature can penetrate historical, political, and linguistic barriers and reach the readership that includes the people of the writer's native country.

As a matter of fact, in our time the intense attachment to one's native land is often viewed as an unnecessary and anachronic feeling that tends to debilitate migrants. I would even argue that, for many displaced people, nostalgia is also blended with fear—the fear of uncertainty and of facing the challenges posed by the larger world and the fear of the absence of the clarity and confidence provided by the past. In essence, nostalgia is associated mostly with the experience of a particular type of migrants, namely, exiles. For most migrants, this attachment can become unreasonable and even unjustified, as the narrator of Salman Rushdie's novel *Shame* refutes: "We know the force of gravity, but not its origins; and to explain why we become attached to our birthplaces we pretend that we are trees and speak of roots. Look under your feet. You will not find gnarled growths sprouting through the soles. Roots, I sometimes think, are a conservative myth, designed to keep us in places."[25] The debunking of the tree metaphor makes it clear that human beings are different from trees and should be rootless and entirely mobile. This is indeed a radical idea, which, in a way, the novel dramatizes, just as its protagonist Omar Khayyam is destroyed after he returns to his native place. But human beings are not always rational animals, and even the same narrator in *Shame* cannot help but feel shamefaced at times and admits, "And to come to the 'roots' idea, I should say that I haven't managed to shake myself free of it completely. Sometimes I do see myself as a tree, even, rather grandly, as the ash Yggdrasil, the mythical world-tree of Norse legend."[26] What is fundamental here is the playfulness manifested in the metaphor of the ash Yggdrasil, which, existing in the domain of Scandinavian mythology, has little to do with the narrator's native place, but which is transplanted into his being through artistic imagination. Thus, art has become his way of reconciliation and transcendence.

The acceptance of rootlessness as one's existential condition—especially by some writers from former British colonies holding a British passport and using English as their first language—exemplifies the situation most migrant writers face. Very few of them are like Solzhenitsyn and Lin Yutang who had been well-established authors before they left their native countries. For most migrant writers today, displacement makes them more vulnerable and their existence more haphazard, since they cannot fall back on any significant past and must struggle to survive in new places. In his novel *The Enigma of Arrival,* V. S. Naipaul poignantly describes such a writer's predicament by reflecting on the eponymous painting by Chirico. The new arrival at a Mediterranean port wanders through the deserted streets and the bazaar of the town, passing strange people and entering mysterious gates to reach the interiors of temples. But finally, exhausted by the adventure and growing forgetful of his mission, he will "get back to the quayside and his ship. But he wouldn't know how." Naipaul writes, "I imagined some religious ritual in which, led on by kindly people, he would unwittingly take part and find himself the intended victim. At the moment of crisis he would come upon a door, open it, and find himself back on the quayside of arrival. He has been saved; the world is as he remembered it. Only one thing is missing now. Above the cutout walls and buildings there is no mast, no sail. The antique ship has gone. The traveler has lived out his life."[27] The depiction of the stranded traveler, to whose arrival Naipaul drew a parallel to his own arrival in England and English literature, speaks allegorically to all the migrants who by chance or by force of circumstances can no longer return to the places of their departures. Their ships are gone, and left on their own in a new place, they have to figure out their bearings and live a life different from that of their past. With the uncertainty that comes with freedom, with the bitterness of betrayal, and with the loneliness intensified by confusion and self-doubt, they will have no choice but to find a way to survive, and, if fortunate, some fulfillment.

Naipaul's portrayal of the writer's predicament is quite poetic despite its melancholy tone of voice. In reality, the struggle is much more painful and maddening. In a letter to his sister Kamla, Naipaul says, "So you will see that the reason why I am remaining in England is really my writing: and I think this is something you will sympathise with, and encourage me. The short-term solution of returning to Trinidad and paying off the debt will cripple all of us in the long run; whereas if I can do something big—with effort—all of us will benefit. Bear with me, I beg you. I am not having it easy: I am not starving, but I worry about my responsibilities towards you a great deal, and I feel ashamed of myself."[28] Naipaul here implores his sister not to ally herself with their mother who wanted him to go home and help the family financially. In addition, he begs his sister to send him money so that he can finish his books in secret. He had told his mother earlier, "I don't see myself fitting into the

Trinidad way of life. I think I shall die if I had to spend the rest of my life in Trinidad."[29] He must have meant an intellectual death in his native country, which, ironically, had offered him the scholarship for Oxford. When he begged for his sister's support, he had written his first two books, but neither had yet been accepted by a publisher. He was a beginning writer and had to justify his literary pursuit even to the people closest to him. To most others, that must have been like courting failure.

How different was Naipaul's situation from that of Solzhenitsyn, who, when banished into exile, had won the Nobel Prize, and from that of Lin Yutang, who, before sailing for America, had written a bestseller in English and had earned the largest royalties ever in China by a single author at the time.[30] It was difficult for Naipaul even to justify his writing to his family, let alone to his native country. It would have been insane for him to think of himself as a spokesman for his people, from whom his emigration to England had obviously alienated him. For a writer like the fledgling Naipaul, he must think how to write well and get published while surviving economically. Any ambition beyond that was a luxury.

I still remember vividly my first reading of Naipaul's novel *A Bend in the River*, a book that changed my life. It was in late December 1992, three years after I had declared in the preface to my first book that I would speak for the unfortunate Chinese, and I was in New York to attend the Modern Language Association convention, hunting for a teaching position. Before this trip, I had looked for a job two years in a row without success. As I walked from hotel to hotel to meet with the interviewers, I could not drive this passage from my mind:

If you look at a column of ants on the march you will see
that there are some who are stragglers or have lost their way.
The column has no time for them; it goes on. Sometimes
the stragglers die. But even this has no effect on the column. There is a little disturbance around the corpse, which
is eventually carried off—and then it appears so light. And
all the time the great busyness continues, and the apparent
sociability, that rite of meeting and greeting which ants trav-
elling in opposite directions, to and from their nest, perform
without fail.[31]

This is how book 2 of the novel begins, when the narrator
laments the death of Father Huismans, a Belgian mission-
ary who collected African masks and carvings, which can
be construed as either preserving the indigenous culture or
looting it. His death is like a ripple in a river that occurs and
then disappears while the stream keeps flowing, just as the
column of ants is undisturbed by the loss of a single member of their tribe. To me, Naipaul's passage captures the
true relationship between the individual and the collective.
Perhaps, that passage pained me even more than Naipaul's
narrator Salim, because people of my generation from mainland China had been indoctrinated to believe that there was
a unstated contract between yourself and your country. As
a citizen, you were supposed to serve your country, and, as
for your livelihood, your country would take care of it for
you. But in America I saw that such a contract gave you a
false sense of entitlement (in China, it would never have occurred to me to look for a job—such an idea was alien to us).
Here you had to work like everyone else to put food on your
table and had to learn to live as an independent man.

Naipaul's novel moved me so much that I wrote two po-

ems in response. One of them is "The Past," and the other
is the following:

In New York City

In the golden rain
I plod along Madison Avenue,
loaded with words.
They are from a page
that shows the insignificance
of a person to a tribe,
just as a hive keeps thriving
while a bee is lost.

On my back the words
are gnawing and gnawing
till they enter into my bones—
I become another man,
alone, wandering,
no longer dreaming of luck
or meeting a friend.

No wisdom shines
like the neon and traffic lights,
but there are words as true as
the money eyes, the yellow cabs,
the fat pigeons on the sills.[32]

As I wandered in downtown Manhattan, those lines echoed
in my mind. They marked the beginning of my doubts about
my claim as a spokesman for the downtrodden Chinese.
Gradually, I came to see the silliness of that ambition.

Naipaul in his essay "Two Worlds" speaks about the necessity of maintaining the distinction between the writer as a social being and the writer who writes. He quotes from Proust's early book *Against Sainte-Beuve* to argue that the self who writes a book is not the same as the person who exists in everyday life.[33] At first glance, this argument against the writer's social functions seems spurious, if not inane. How many significant writers have promoted justice with their pens? How many of them have been regarded as a conscience of the people? Some have even endeavored to save the soul of a nation. The assumption is that to become a good writer you have to be a good person, that the writing person and social being are one. But if we examine the issue, we see that both Proust and Naipaul are right. Even the most socially conscientious writers like Solzhenitsyn and Lin Yutang could be accepted by their peoples only on the grounds that they had written lasting literary works. Their social functions in their lifetimes have been largely forgotten; what remains are the books secreted from their writing selves. This is a cliché but still holds true: a writer's first responsibility is to write well. His social role is only secondary, mostly given by the forces around him, and it has little to do with his value as a writer.

On several occasions, I said I would stop writing about contemporary China. People often asked me, "Why burn your bridges?" or "Why mess with success?" I would reply, "My heart is no longer there." In retrospect, I can see that my decision to leave contemporary China in my writing is a way to negate the role of the spokesmanship I used to envision for myself. I must learn to stand alone, as a writer.

That said, I do not mean that a writer should live in an ivory tower, answerable only to his art. I can even admire those writers, portrayed by Nadine Gordimer in her essay "The Essential Gesture," who have managed to function as both a writer and an activist and whose art responds to social exigencies. Before I turned to writing seriously at the age of thirty-two, I had never planned to become a writer. During my first eight years of college teaching, I never used the word "art" in the classroom, having my doubts about writing as an art, not to mention its value, its integrity, its autonomy, and its effectiveness in shaping society, though I had kept writing poetry and fiction. I could agree with Gordimer wholeheartedly that a writer must be "more than a writer" and must be responsible to the well-being of his fellow citizens.[34] For a long time, I was deeply moved by Derek Walcott's line in "The Schooner Flight": "either I'm nobody, or I'm a nation."[35] However, as I continued writing, the issue of the writer's essential gesture as a social being grew more complicated to me. Writers do not make good generals, and today literature is ineffective at social change. All the writer can strive for is a personal voice.

But for whom does the writer speak? Of course not just for himself. Then, for a group? For those who are not listened to? There is no argument that the writer must take a moral stand and speak against oppression, prejudice, and injustice, but such a gesture must be secondary, and he should be aware of the limits of his art as social struggle. His real battlefield is nowhere but on the page. His work will be of little value if not realized as art. Surveying contemporary history, both of the East and West, we can see many blank spaces unmarked by literature: genocides, wars, political upheavals, and manmade catastrophes. Take the example of the Anti-Rightist Movement in China in the late 1950s. Millions of people suffered persecution, tens of thousands of intellectuals were sent to the hinterlands and perished there, yet not a single piece of literature with lasting value emerged from this historical calamity. The victims were the best educated in Chinese society, and some of them are still alive but too old to produce any significant work. Many of the accused Rightists were both writers and activists, and some still write petitions and articles and organize conferences. But without a lasting literary work, their sufferings and losses will fade considerably in the collective memory, if not altogether. Is that not a great loss? What was needed was one artist who could stay above immediate social needs and create a genuine piece of literature that preserved the oppressed in memory. Yes, to preserve is the key function of literature, which, to combat historical amnesia, must be predicated on the autonomy and integrity of literary works inviolable by time. In Andrei Makine's *Dreams of My Russian Summers,* the narrator meditates on how to bear witness: "And they [the Russians who were busy writing personal memoirs] did not understand that history had no need for all these innumerable little Gulags. A single monumental one, recognized as a classic, sufficed."[36] As this implies, the writer should be not just a chronicler but also a shaper, an alchemist, of historical experiences.

The writer should enter history mainly through the avenue of his art. If he serves a cause or a group or even a country, such a service must be a self-choice and not imposed by society. He must serve on his own terms, in the manner and at the time and place of his own choosing. Whatever role he plays, he must keep in mind that his success or failure as a writer will be determined only on the page. That is the space where he should strive to exist.

The Language of Betrayal

The antonym of "betrayal" is "loyalty" or "allegiance." Uneasy about those words, the migrant writer feels guilty because of his physical absence from his native country, which is conventionally viewed by some of his countrymen as "desertion." Yet the ultimate betrayal is to choose to write in another language. No matter how the writer attempts to rationalize and justify adopting a foreign language, it is an act of betrayal that alienates him from his mother tongue and directs his creative energy to another language. This linguistic betrayal is the ultimate step the migrant writer dares to take; after this, any other act of estrangement amounts to a trifle.

Historically, it has always been the individual who is accused of betraying his country. Why shouldn't we turn the tables by accusing a country of betraying the individual? Most countries have been such habitual traitors to their citizens anyway. The worst crime the country commits against the writer is to make him unable to write with honesty and artistic integrity.

As long as he can, a writer will stay within his mother tongue, his safe domain. The German writer W. G. Sebald lived and taught in England for over three decades and knew both English and French well, but he always wrote in his native language. When asked why he had not switched to English, he answered there was no necessity. That he could give such an answer must be because German was a major European language from which his works could be rendered into other European languages without much difficulty. In contrast, the Franco-Czech writer Milan Kundera started writing in French when he was already over sixty. Such a heroic effort might signify some crisis that prompted the novelist to make the drastic switch. If we compared Kundera's recent fiction written in French with his earlier books written in Czech, we can see that the recent prose, after *Immortality,* is much thinner. Nevertheless, his adopting French is a brave literary adventure pursued with a relentless spirit. Just as the narrator of his novel *Ignorance* regards Odysseus's return to Ithaca as accepting "the finitude of life,"[1] Kundera cannot turn back and continues his odyssey. That also explains why he has referred to France as his "second homeland."

I have been asked why I write in English. I often reply, "For survival." People tend to equate "survival" with "livelihood" and praise my modest, also shabby, motivation. In fact, physical survival is just one side of the picture, and there is the other side, namely, to exist—to live a meaningful life. To exist also means to make the best use of one's life, to pursue one's vision. Joseph Brodsky once observed,

"When a writer resorts to a language other than his mother tongue, he does so either out of necessity, like Conrad, or because of burning ambition, like Nabokov, or for the sake of greater estrangement, like Beckett."[2] Brodsky's clear demarcation of the three writers' motivations is a way to introduce the topic of his erudite essay "To Please a Shadow," but in reality, a writer's motivations are mixed. In a writer who migrates to another language, necessity, ambition, and estrangement usually come to bear at the same time. Nabokov often said Russian was a dying language, so out of necessity he had begun writing in English even before he emigrated to the United States. Although his works are apolitical on the whole, he admits, "I am aware of a central core of spirit in me that flashes and jeers at the brutal farce of totalitarian states, such as Russia, and her embarrassing tumors, such as China."[3] Clearly, further estrangement from Soviet Russia was Nabokov's motivation too.

Conrad often gave the impression of writing under the pressure of necessity. In fact, the ambition to become a significant writer was always part of his vision. We know he regarded Flaubert as his master and Henry James as his peer. To realize his ambition, he had no choice but to write in a major European language—English—though he never felt at ease with his decision. Throughout his productive years, especially during the First World War, he frequently got involved in the affairs of Poland to support its struggle against Russian tyranny. He stated that one of his literary ambitions was to write about the Polish experience, though he managed to do that only in a few short stories, such as "Prince Roman" and "Amy Foster."

On his visit to Poland in 1914 after an absence of twenty-one years, Conrad was anxious despite his international reputation, afraid his native country might give him the cold shoulder. Ironically, in England, he always felt like a foreigner and was viewed as one as well. That must be one of the reasons he declined the honorary degrees offered by Oxford, Cambridge, and other universities, and also a knighthood from the British government (in 1924). What he really wanted was the Nobel Prize, for which he was never officially nominated. On the one hand, his refusals of those British honors seemed to indicate his determination to remain independent; on the other, I believe, the refusals might also suggest that he wanted to become a European writer, to have an identity inclusive of both the British and the Polish. In other words, he wanted the international prize to mend the division within his identity. The Nobel Prize would also have brought honor to the Poles and therefore would have redeemed him from the guilt for his "desertion" of Poland, never mind that his emigration was entirely justified—if he had remained in the Polish region occupied by Russians, he would have been forced to serve in the invaders' army for many years.[4] Conrad's eagerness for the international prize verged on naïveté. He confided to his young disciple Jean-Aubry: "Yeats has had the Nobel Prize. My opinion about that is that it is a literary recognition of the new Irish Free State (that's what it seems to me), but that does not destroy my chances of getting it in one or two years."[5] Conrad was surprised when the prize went to an inferior Polish writer, Wladyslaw Reymont, in 1924, the year he hoped to receive it. He did not realize that he represented no country.

However, time has been fair to Conrad. Since his death, he has become one of the most popular writers in Poland. His stories have been included in school textbooks. He has grown into a mystical figure in Polish culture and has been celebrated as one of its heroes, though probably the most solitary and misunderstood one. Polish poets have been particularly fascinated by him, perhaps because he evokes in them the guilty glamour of exile. According to Adam Gillon, almost half of contemporary Polish poets have written about Conrad's emigration and about his attachment to his roots, and some have even portrayed him, a seaman by profession, as a modern Odysseus who never made it back to his original shore. The poet Stanislaw Mlodozeniec (1929–) addresses the itinerant hero in his "A Song about Conrad" as follows:

> You have tamed the distant lands and seas,
> The treacherous currents of the deep
> With the twist of foreign speech.
> You threaded the wide world
> Upon the bleeding Polish soul.
> Those alien seas—they are ours.
> Your ghost is wandering everywhere,
> A familiar footprint on the alien seas.
> The wind is blowing with your breath.

Even Conrad's inability to go back to his native country is idealized as a way toward deeper significance and eventually toward a kind of metaphysical return, which will reach not his native land but a distant origin shared by humanity. Krysztof Jezewski (1939–) eulogizes in his poem "Joseph Conrad Leaves Poland":

> When the lips of darkness swallowed
> your bleeding and tattered land,
> when you were left alone

you took the world into your breast, like air into your
    lungs,
and the return was there, always at the far-flung shore—
the infinite abyss—
of the sea
and of Man.[6]

With courage and endurance, the lonely sea-battered
Conrad made his conquest in English letters. After his
death, the Poles gradually embraced him as one of their own
just as the English had, precisely because he is such an original spirit that no single nation can contain him.

For the moment, allow me to be a spoilsport. Let me
remind you of a disgraceful page in Polish literature that
stunned our hero and plagued him for many years. The April
1899 issue of *Kraj* (Homeland), a Polish journal published in
St. Petersburg, brought out an article, by Eliza Orzeszkowa
(1841–1910), the grande dame of the Polish literary circle,
about Conrad, who had published four books in English but
was hardly known to the Poles. Orzeszkowa condemned
him vehemently:

And since we talked about books, I must say that the gentleman who in English is writing novels which are widely read
and bring good profit almost caused me a nervous attack.
When reading about him, I felt something slippery and un-
pleasant, something mounting to my throat. Really! That
even creative talents should join the exodus! Till now we
have talked only about engineers and operatic singers! But
now we should give absolution to a writer! . . . Creative ability is the very crown of the plant, the very top of the tower,
the very heart of the heart of the nation. And to take away

from one's nation this flower, this top, this heart and to give
it to the Anglo-Saxons who are not even lacking in bird's
milk, for the only reason that they pay better for it—one
cannot even think of it without shame. And what is still
worse, the gentleman bears the name of his perhaps very
near relative, that Joseph Korzeniowski over whose novels
I shed as a young girl the first tears of sympathy and felt the
first ardors of noble enthusiasms and decisions. Over the
novels of Mr. Conrad Korzeniowski no Polish girl will shed
an altruistic tear or take a noble decision. But on second
thought, this causes me only moderate grief, because believ-
ing in the superiority of the elements of which all creative
power is composed, I do not suppose that our writers would
ever embrace the profession of a vivandiere or a huckster.
Besides, we do not starve even if we remain in our place,
that we should need to feed on the crumbs from the table
of great lords. In this respect we ourselves are *seigneurs* great
enough.[7]

I have quoted Orzeszkowa at length to show the full
range of her accusations. They are basically threefold: first,
Conrad's emigration is a desertion of his native country, because he should have remained in Poland and let his creative
talent serve the Polish national cause—in today's terminol-
ogy, his emigration was "voluntary brain drain"; second,
to write in English is an act of betrayal, since conventionally to write in Polish was viewed as a patriotic act; third,
to make money by writing in a major and powerful foreign
language is to reduce the writer to the level of a peddler,
which in turn will make the writer's work insignificant to
his own people. To humiliate Conrad further, Orzeszkowa
shrewdly mentions his real family name "Korzeniowski" to

conjure up the ghost of his father, Apollo Korzeniowski, a minor literary figure and a well-known hotheaded patriot. Note that she only "read about"—not actually read—Conrad's books and could not possibly know about the quality and content of his fiction. Worse, she presented him as an affluent man, which contradicts the fact that he was in dire financial straits at the time. In essence, hers is a collective voice, which demands the writer's unconditional dedication and sacrifice but does not care whether he could survive in a foreign land. It is a voice that disregards the individual's particular circumstances.

Conrad did have his defenders, and the best known one was Wincenty Lutoslawski, a philosopher who had emigrated to the United States in 1896 and lived in Boston for some time. From Henry James, Lutoslawski heard about Conrad and later visited him while staying in England in 1897. In the same issue of *Kraj* that carried Orzeszkowa's article, he argued that the Polish nation should not discourage the strong ones among its population from moving abroad to fully develop their talents, because the emigrants will never forget or betray their native land and instead will spread Polish influence throughout the world. On that account, they will also serve the country. Lutoslawski must have been a nuisance to Conrad, though the philosopher continued standing beside him for over a decade. On two occasions, he asked Conrad why he did not write in Polish. On the first one, Conrad seemed to beg the question, saying, "Sir, I hold our beautiful Polish literature in too high esteem to introduce to it my poor writing. But for the English my abilities are sufficient and secure my daily bread." Three years later, Conrad responded to the same question from Lutoslawski in the same vein, "To write in Polish! That's a great thing, for that one must be a writer like Mickiewicz or Krasinski. I am a common man, I write to earn my living and to support my wife, in the language of the country where I found refuge."[8] Incapable of sound literary judgment, Lutoslawski took Conrad's words at face value and went on carrying the torch of defending his fellow emigrant. In his book *Sparks of Warsaw* (1911), twelve years after the initial attack on Conrad, Lutoslawski continued to spar with Orzeszkowa to justify Conrad's choosing to write in English. However, he reached such a ludicrous conclusion: "Let us not envy the English for a second rate writer, who anyway would not have enriched our literature, since he himself avows that profit was the motive of his creative activity. We are rich enough to give many such writers to all the nations of the earth and retain for ourselves only the best ones who will express their souls in Polish."[9]

Indeed, it is difficult to recognize a genius when we know him personally. We are not sure how Conrad came to know about Orzeszkowa's attack, but we do know that Orzeszkowa had the temerity to write Conrad soon afterward and might have enclosed a copy of her article. Conrad, who held fidelity as the first principle of life,[10] was incensed and confused, probably wounded as well, and he never forgot the insult. On his visit to Poland fifteen years later, in 1914, he read as much Polish literature as he could lay his hands on. A cousin of his inadvertently offered him a novel by Orzeszkowa, and Conrad burst out: "Don't dare to bring me that! . . . You don't know, she once wrote me such a letter."[11] Yet despite his anger, publicly he was always reticent about the Polish attack on him.

However, in private and in a roundabout way, he did respond to it. In a letter to historian Jozef Korzeniowski in February 1901, Conrad wrote,

> And please let me add, dear Sir (for you may still be hearing this and that said of me), that I have in no way disavowed either my nationality or the name we share for the sake of success [Korzeniowski is not a relative to Conrad despite their same last name]. It is widely known that I am a Pole and that Jozef Konrad are my two Christian names, the latter being used by me as a surname so that foreign mouths should not distort my real surname—a distortion which I cannot stand. It does not seem to me that I have been unfaithful to my country by having proved to the English that a gentleman from the Ukraine can be as good a sailor as they, and has something to tell them in their own language.[12]

Evidently, Conrad was in total earnest about his loyalty to his native country and to the name of his family. Interestingly enough, he put "sailor" before "writer" in terms of his achievements. By 1901, he had published his masterpiece *Lord Jim* and four other novels and should have been more confident in presenting himself as a writer. Then why didn't he just speak about his authorship in his letter to the historian as his justification? Why did he foreground his seamanship instead?

To be an effective sailor, in Conrad's case a captain, one has to be responsible and trustworthy—the seaman's professional honor and code of conduct do not permit any suspicion of unfaithfulness. For the same reason, in his autobiography, *A Personal Record* (1908), Conrad elaborates on his reliability as a seaman to convince the reader that he is a loyal man. Once on this line of argument, he can hardly refrain from indulging his pen, as if a decade after Orzeszkowa's attack, he finally has a chance to respond.[13]

Actually, making the case for writing in English is difficult for Conrad. There is no way to prove the writer's loyalty to the Polish nation if his subject matter has no bearing on Poland, not to mention being written in a language the Poles cannot read, so the most Conrad can say in his letter to the historian is that he has something interesting to tell the English in their own language. His argument sounds unconvincing. We know that "betrayal" is a major theme in Conrad's fiction. A character like the guilty Tuan Jim can deliver himself to Chief Doramin as a desperate measure of self-redemption, or one like the dying Nostromo can come clean about the stolen silver to Mrs. Gould, but how can the accused author redeem himself if he does not kill himself out of mad guilt caused by his own decision to write in a foreign language but instead persists in making books in English? Conrad seemed unable to find an appropriate way to defend himself as a writer and thus chose to remain reticent publicly.

He was in a painful but original position, though he might not have been fully aware of its significance. Today, if an accusation of linguistic betrayal is launched against a writer who has adopted English, he can cite Conrad as a precedent to justify his choice. He can even claim he is working within the tradition founded by Conrad, in which some nonnative speakers became essential writers in this language. But before Conrad there had been no Conrad in English, and Joseph Conrad had to grapple with the blame and guilt alone. His agony was part of the price he paid for his originality.

In literature, some writers have achieved permanence not only because they produced significant works but also because they emerged at the right time. Conrad is such a significant writer that his timely appearance in English is apt to overshadow those who arrive after him. We cannot but regard him as a founding spirit.

Where Conrad's works are concerned, some later writers would not acknowledge him as a master of the art of fiction. They often felt uncomfortable about being compared to him. In his essay "Conrad's Darkness and Mine," V. S. Naipaul speaks extensively about Conrad's inadequacy as a fiction writer despite acknowledging his debt to him:

> My reservations about Conrad as a novelist remain. There is something flawed and unexercised about his creative imagination. He does not — except in *Nostromo* and some of the stories — involve me in his fantasy; and *Lord Jim* is still to me more acceptable as a narrative poem than as a novel. Conrad's value to me is that he is someone who sixty to seventy years ago mediated on my world, a world I recognize today. I feel this about no other writer of the century.[14]

Naipaul is partly right about Conrad's prose style, which tends to be purple at the expense of immediacy and penetrativeness. Indeed, some of his novels and stories often read like prose poetry, which can be a virtue, and some of his main characters, often flat, remain underdeveloped. Even his masterpiece *Heart of Darkness* suffers from lack of dramatic complications. Nonetheless, Conrad is not a writer we can judge only by technique. He stands as a monument. I believe Naipaul is mistaken about *Lord Jim*. The last quarter of the novel is charged with suspense, pathos, and dramatic intensity. To my mind, there is no doubt that it is a magnificent novel written with tremendous skill and subtlety. Above all, it has depth and complexity.

In some of his fiction, Conrad depends on the gravity of the subject matter and the tension of the dramatic situation to hold the story together, such as in "Typhoon," "Youth," "The Secret Sharer," and *The Nigger of the "Narcissus."* But this does not mean that he didn't know how to create dramatic complications to charge his fiction with narrative momentum. Some of his masterpieces, such as "An Outpost of Progress," *Lord Jim,* and *Nostromo,* have dramatic complications in abundance, handled ingeniously. Any writer who can create fiction of this caliber knows the craft inside out. In other words, Conrad's choice of relying on thematic gravity and dramatic tension more than on dramatic complications may demonstrate his confidence in his art, which might purposely have excluded some conventional fiction techniques.

As far as the use of the English language goes, Naipaul has a good reason to distance himself from Conrad, since English is Naipaul's first language, not posing the same challenge to him as to Conrad. His affiliation with Conrad is mainly thematic as he acknowledged. Conrad opened a territory for him and inspired his literary imagination. In addition, Naipaul writes about the same themes as Conrad did, namely, the mingling of races and the meeting of cultures. For that reason, whether he likes it or not, Naipaul is viewed as "Conrad's heir."[15]

Nabokov, despising big ideas in fiction as "hogwash," resents being compared to Conrad for a different reason, which is primarily linguistic. In an interview in January 1964, he said, "I cannot abide Conrad's souvenir-shop style, bottled ships and shell necklaces of romanticist cliches."[16]

In truth, we—writers who have adopted English—are all related to Conrad one way or another; even Nabokov is no exception. Aside from the possibility of having in mind Conrad's tussle with the Russian masters, as he did in *The Secret Agent* with Tolstoy and in *Under Western Eyes* with Dostoevsky, Nabokov disparages Conrad mainly to differentiate himself from him stylistically. What he refers to in the interview is the kind of neutral English Conrad used, though Nabokov's remarks are somewhat off the mark. Conrad's English, neutral as it is, has its unique strength and stark elegance. It often rises to the level of poetry, as in this paragraph from "An Outpost of Progress" depicting the ominous surroundings of a trading station in Africa:

> There was some talk about keeping a watch in turn, but in the evening everything seemed so quiet and peaceful that they retired as usual. All night they were disturbed by a lot of drumming in the villages. A deep, rapid roll near by would be followed by another far off—then all ceased. Soon short appeals would rattle out here and there, then all mingle together, increase, become vigorous and sustained, would spread out over the forest, roll through the night, unbroken and ceaseless, near and far, as if the whole land had been one immense drum booming out steadily an appeal to heaven. And through the deep and tremendous noise sudden yells that resembled snatches of songs from a madhouse darted shrill and high in discordant jets of sound which seemed to rush far above the earth and drive all peace from under the stars.[17]

Few readers can fail to see the power and beauty of the language in this passage (passages like this can be found practically in any piece of fiction by Conrad). The language shows that there is enough room in Conrad's neutral English for realizing his art fully. Staying within this kind of language, Conrad does not need to write anything untranslatable, just as his subject matter is generally international.

Despite his determination to be entirely original, Nabokov still had to take on the task of how to do more than Conrad in English. That he tried to present himself as absolutely unrelated to Conrad reveals his anxiety about being overshadowed by his predecessor. Nabokov tried to do two things in English to outshine Conrad—one was to write poetry and the other was to create a distinct prose style of his own. His poetic effort was resolute but did not succeed completely. Soon after arrival in America in 1940, he began to publish his English poems in the *New Yorker,* fourteen of them over the years. As he translated Pushkin's *Eugene Onegin* in the 1950s, he also studied English metrics and eventually wrote a lengthy appendix to the translation on the meter/rhythm approaches in both Russian and English poetics. Later, this appendix was published as a book entitled *Notes on Prosody.*[18] In it, Nabokov intends to correct, if not overhaul, English prosody by introducing into it the concept of skud and tilt. A skud refers to a pyrrhic foot (a bisyllabic foot without a stress), while a tilt refers to a bisyllabic foot with a misplaced stress. Evidently, a tilt is not much different from a trochee and does not deserve elaborate treatment. On the other hand, Nabokov's insistence on adopting the skud could indeed have refined English prosody if his theory were accepted, because English prosody does not deal with the weak pyrrhic foot. But he was too aggressive and too ambitious in propounding his prosodic theory, and as a result, the significance of his treatise has been neglected or ignored.[19]

His effort to become a poet in English culminated in *Pale Fire* (1962), the novel whose main part consists of 999 lines of poetry, in heroic couplets and four cantos. Comparing the fictional Charles Kinbote's prose foreword with John Shade's poetry, we can see that the prose is by far superior to the poetry in the novel. The prose is full of subtlety and humor, whereas the poetry is laborious and clunky, at times opaque. The lines are straitjacketed in pentameters without variation. Nabokov didn't seem to know how to play with the metrics to produce dramatic effects, and apparently, he is a great prose master but a mediocre poet in English.[20]

Among his English poems, the best one is "A Discovery," a piece about his lepidopterological experience. The first two stanzas describe a butterfly this way:

> I found it in a legendary land
> all rocks and lavender and tufted grass,
> where it was settled on some sodden sand
> hard by the torrent of a mountain pass.

> The features it combines mark it as new
> to science: shape and shade—the special tinge,
> akin to moonlight, tempering its blue,
> the dingy underside, the checquered fringe.[21]

As poetry, that is good enough. But let us look at a prose passage that he wrote also about butterflies:

A score of small butterflies, all of one kind, were settled on
a damp patch of sand, their wings erect and closed, showing
their pale undersides with dark dots and tiny orange-rimmed
peacock spots along the hindwing margins; one of Pnin's
shed rubbers disturbed some of them and revealing the ce-
lestial hue of their upper surface, they fluttered around like
blue snowflakes before settling again.[22]

By comparison, the prose is more poetic than the poetry.
The passage from *Pnin* is lively and radiant in contrast to
the gloomy, ponderous lines of the poem. Rhymes and feet
alone do not make poetry, which requires a burst of energy
in its articulation. On the whole, Nabokov's English poems lack lyrical intensity and dynamic motion, the essential qualities of effective poetry. At times, he tried hard to
make words sound as rich and rhythmic as possible, mainly
via alliterations and assonances, but his verbal sounds rarely
echo the senses. More problematic, there is no spontaneity
in his lines. In poetic composition, one of the fundamental
principles is effortlessness, as Yeats enunciates in "Adam's
Curse": "Yet if it does not seem a moment's thought, / Our
stitching and unstitching has been naught." Nabokov's English poetry seldom moves with that kind of assuredness.

In fact, Nabokov himself might have been aware of this
defect. When asked by an interviewer, "Do you feel you
have any conspicuous or secret flaw as a writer?" Nabokov
admitted:

The absence of a natural vocabulary. An odd thing to con-
fess, but true. Of the two instruments in my possession,
one—my native tongue—I can no longer use, and this not

only because I lack a Russian audience, but also because the excitement of verbal adventure in the Russian medium has faded away gradually after I turned to English in 1940. My English, this second instrument I have always had, is however a stiffish, artificial thing, which may be all right for describing a sunset or an insect, but which cannot conceal poverty of syntax and paucity of domestic diction when I need the shortest road between warehouse and shop. An old Rolls-Royce is not always preferable to a plain Jeep.[23]

Despite his emphasis on his difference from Conrad, Nabokov here reveals a Conradian plight—that is, his departure from his mother tongue crippled him linguistically. In general, he would not voice this pain explicitly, yet here is a clear admission: "My complete switch from Russian prose to English prose was exceedingly painful—like learning anew to handle things after losing seven or eight fingers in an explosion."[24] We can see that he suffered from the same affliction as Conrad.

Nonetheless, Nabokov is a grand master of English prose and did manage to outshine Conrad stylistically. Neither of them, lacking the natural idiom, could write dialogue in a spontaneous manner,[25] but they knew how to turn their "handicaps" to their advantage. Understandably, their fiction relies heavily on the narrative style. Conrad developed an elaborate, vigorous syntax that differentiates him from his contemporaries, though his unique style lacks playfulness. He did not make jokes. By contrast, Nabokov was determined to be playful in his fiction. His playfulness consists of humor, wit, word games, endless wisecracks. His delightful stylistic innovation not only assures him an original place

in modern fiction but also alters the landscape of the literature written by authors who migrated to English.

Conventionally, playfulness was a taboo to writers who
adopted a foreign language. Stanislaw Baranczak, the Harvard professor of Polish language and literature, discusses
this issue in his essay "Tongue-Tied Eloquence: Notes
on Language, Exile, and Writing." He argues that linguistic playfulness is impossible to accomplish for an exiled
writer who chooses to write in another language partly because he speaks to an audience in his adopted country who
have different cultural and linguistic references and cannot fully understand him. He cites the example of a famous Eastern European wit Antoni Slonimski, who fled
to England when the Second World War broke out but
went back to the socialist Poland in 1951 simply because
every joke he cracked to the English had been a flop. Professor Baranczak concludes that the most the exiled writer
can achieve is fluency—to get his messages across—in another language, no more than that. Therefore, this stylistic
limitation prevents the writer from producing genuine literature. His warning sounds reasonable, authoritative, and
disheartening:

> True, even though the absolutely perfect command of a lan-
> guage is something an outsider cannot really acquire, he can,
> through a lot of effort, finally attain a fluency and glibness
> that makes him sound almost like a native writer. But lit-
> erature is something more than glib writing. It also includes
> the right—and necessity—to violate glibness, to make light
> of rules, to speak in a novel way without bothering to be
> correct. In literature, a new thought cannot emerge except

from a new way of speaking: in order to say anything relevant, you must break a norm. And this is precisely what an
outsider cannot afford, since if breaking is to make any sense
at all, you may break only the norms that bind you, not those
that bind someone else. If a native writer purposely violates
language, it's called progress; if an outsider does it, it's called
malapropism.[26]

Curiously enough, Professor Baranczak left Nabokov out of
his discussion, perhaps because the novelist was trilingual
and actually spoke English in his infancy. All the same, as I
have observed, Nabokov faced the same linguistic challenge
as Conrad, namely, "what to make of a diminished thing."
On the one hand, Nabokov had to settle for "a second-rate
brand of English," and, on the other, he was determined
to "scale . . . verbal peaks," climbing higher than Conrad's
"readymade English" could ever reach.[27] He understood his
limitations and disadvantages and construed the language
problem differently from Professor Baranczak's analyses.
For him, what was essential was to find his own position
in English, which needed to be unconventional (and even
alien). In the words of the narrator of *Pnin,* "Genius is non-
conformity."[28]

Nabokov kicked the strictures against playfulness to
pieces. From the very beginning, he used English with little
regard for rules. Edmund Wilson, as an editor of the *New
Republic,* wrote to him in one of his early letters: "do please
refrain from puns, to which I see you have a slight propen-
sity. They are pretty much excluded from serious journal-
ism here."[29] Wilson, a man of letters, understood the value
of playfulness in literature and discouraged Nabokov from
indulging in word games in functional prose. Yet Nabokov

never mended his ways. Even in his nonfiction, he would not stop cracking jokes. He would toss out expressions like "how time crawls!" "I miss America—even Miss America," and "in the so-called literary circles where I seldom revolve," as if he always squinted at the words he inscribed on paper to see what extra pleasure he could extract from them. He seized every opportunity to turn self-consciousness into delightful art.

His work differs from Conrad's precisely in his nonchalant verbal playfulness, which constitutes a part of his contribution to English. There are several kinds of playfulness in his language, and the most hard-earned are word games. For example, in *Pnin,* a novel verbally more adventurous than *Lolita,* the narrator keeps making fun of the bookish protagonist, using hilarious phrases and sentences, such as "On the third hand (these mental states sprout additional forelimbs all the time)," "a curriculum vitae in a nutshell—a coconut shell," "Pnin served the cocktails 'or better to say flamingotails—specially for ornithologists,'" "you made me the honor to interrogate me," and "Pnin declared he was shot when he was fired from his job."[30] These verbal feats are not puns that mostly operate on phonetic echoes, nor are they the kind of wisecracks that a native speaker can bring off easily. They are unique to a nonnative speaker who has an alien perspective on English and is easily amazed by the most common features of his adopted language. They belong to a space in English that Nabokov opened mainly for nonnative writers. His word games are of a different order, more exciting and more original—based on the misuse and distortion of words and grammar and often originating from mistakes.[31] After Nabokov, who can say nonnative writers cannot crack jokes in English?

In Nabokov's fiction, word games are just one kind of playfulness with language that he exploits to humorous effect. Nabokov made the best use of his polyglotism and produced humor that originates from the interplay of languages. When asked about the advantages of being able to write in several languages, he replied, "The ability to render an exact nuance by shifting from the language I am now using to a brief burst of French or to a soft rustle of Russian."[32] I don't read Russian and can't see how he achieved this in action with that language, but I can see some of his marvelous performances in connection with French. Pnin, a Russian exile or immigrant (I view his as an immigrant) who knows French, speaks this sort of English at a train station after he realizes he took the wrong train:

> "Important lecture!" cried Pnin. "What to do? It is a
> cata-troph!"
>
> [He left his bag with the clerk.]
>
> "Quittance?" queried Pnin, Englishing the Russian for "receipt."
> "What's that?"
> "Number?" tried Pnin.
> "You don't need a number," said the fellow, and resumed his
> writing.
>
> [Later Pnin returned to collect his bag]
>
> "But I must obtain my valise!" cried Pnin.[33]

Pnin's English is mixed with French and Russian words. He has only a bookish vocabulary in English, calling his "stone-heavy bag" "my valise." Whenever he is desperate, all kinds of foreign words will pop up in his wild English. These foreign words intensify the plight that trapped Pnin, who often stumbles in hunting for proper English words when he speaks. The syncopated word "cata-troph" in the above dialogue is actually a hybrid that belongs to neither English nor French. The mispronunciation not only gives pleasure to the reader but also conveys the pain of the immigrant who has to struggle in the new language every day, sometimes hopelessly.

Some of the jokes that originate from the interplay of languages may not be easy to catch, since they are more subtle and refined. When Joan Clements shows Pnin the room he wants to rent, Pnin holds "his hands a little distance from the window" and asks,

> "Is temperature uniform?"
> Joan dashed to the radiator.
> "Piping hot," she reported.
> "I am asking—are there currents of air?"
> "Oh yes, you will have plenty of air. And here is the bathroom—
>   small, but all yours."
> "No *douche?*" inquired Pnin, looking up. "Maybe it is better so."[34]

The monolingual landlady misunderstands the phrase "currents of air," a verbatim translation of the French idiom *courants d'air,* which here should mean "cold wind from the cracks of the window—a draft." Instead, she takes the phrase as a reference to the ventilation of the room. But the reader can perceive the miscommunication, which is funny though not totally transparent. Such frustration must be commonplace in the nonnative speaker Pnin's everyday life, so he does not bother to correct Joan further. Again, when he uses the word *douche,* which means "shower" in both French and Russian, Pnin realizes that Joan didn't follow the meaning, but he gives up trying to get it across and instead says, "Maybe it is better so." Again, the joke may not be caught by Pnin's interlocutor, but some readers can detect it. This is a good example of Nabokov's uncompromising style, which never condescends to cater to the general audience's taste or to compensate for its facile comprehension.

When Pnin is happy, his jokes—whether made purposely or inadvertently—tend to be brighter and often hilarious. Later in the story, Pnin invites Professor Thomas to his party with this little speech: "So I take the opportunity to extend a cordial invitation to you to visit me this evening. Half past eight, postmeridian. A little house-heating soiree, nothing more. Bring also your spouse—or perhaps you are a Bachelor of Hearts?"[35] This is lovely. Pnin's joyful mood often makes his verbal mistakes warm and brilliant.

In his essay on the exiled writer's linguistic predicament, Professor Baranczak does not offer samples of misfired jokes, which I assume must belong to the category of wordplay. In fact, jokes do not always come from language alone, especially in the case of witticisms, which can arise from dramatic situations or from peculiar ways of saying things. In other words, humor does not have to be strictly language bound. The Chinese humorist Lin Yutang once announced before speaking at a meeting, "A speech should be like a miniskirt—the shorter, the better." On other occasions, he was humorous as well: "I cannot say my writings are not good"; "Where there are too many lawyers, there is no justice"; "Our lives are not in the hands of the Lord but in the hands of chefs"; "How could imagination soar on the clipped wings of a drab, non-smoking soul?"; and "The wisest man is therefore he who loafs most gracefully." These witticisms translate well. They are so self-contained that even if they are taken out of context, their meanings remain intact.

But this kind of witticism belongs mainly to nonfiction. In fiction, humor should arise from within the drama and should be acted out by characters. Nabokov's fiction is marked by a peculiar humor that is Gogolian by nature, though Nabokov himself might not have been willing to acknowledge this. When teaching at Wellesley College, he graded the classical Russian authors for his students: Tolstoy got an A plus, whereas Dostoyevsky was debased with a C minus, and Gogol—on whom Nabokov wrote a thought-provoking book in English in 1944—was given a B minus.[36] He seemed to judge writers purely by aesthetics. In fact, literature is not only a matter of technique but also a matter of spirit—many great works are technically flawed, but their flaws do not seriously diminish their significance. Despite Nabokov's low opinion of Gogol, if we carefully examine *Dead Souls* and *Pnin,* we can see that Nabokov learned quite a bit from Gogol. In addition to the comic treatment of the tragic little-man protagonist, there is a kind of dramatic playfulness that is fantastic and even perverse, and clearly Gogolian. Like Gogol, Nabokov managed to create magic out of nothing substantial. Let me cite two hilarious passages to illustrate this miraculous playfulness:

It warmed my heart, the Russian-intelligentski way he [Pnin] had of getting into his overcoat: his inclined head would demonstrate its ideal baldness, and his large, Duchess of Wonderland chin would firmly press against the crossed ends of his green muffler to hold it in place on his chest while, with a jerk of his broad shoulders, he contrived to get into both armholes at once; another heave and the coat was on.[37]

Pnin's putting on his overcoat is a very mundane detail that usually would not deserve an elaborate description. Most writers would describe such an act with one short sentence or a phrase, but Nabokov's narrator presents it elaborately, with gusto and rapture, making a huge fuss about a trifle. Here is another passage that shows how Pnin feels after his teeth were pulled:

A warm flow of pain was gradually replacing the ice and wood of the anesthetic in his thawing, still half dead, abominably martyred mouth. After that, during a few days he was in mourning for an intimate part of himself. It surprised him to realize how fond he had been of his teeth. His tongue, a fat sleek seal, used to flop and slide so happily among the familiar rocks, checking the contours of a battered but still secure kingdom, plunging from cave to cove, climbing this jag, nuzzling that notch, finding a shred of sweet seaweed in the same old cleft; but now not a landmark remained, and all there existed was a great dark wound, a terra incognita of gums which dread and disgust forbade one to investigate.[38]

The way those trivial details—putting on an overcoat and having had one's teeth extracted—are fantastically observed is similar to the way the distant barking dogs are portrayed as various types of musicians in chapter 3 of *Dead Souls*.[39] This kind of playfulness, based on the disproportionate presentation of trivial details, is not confined to any specific language and has more to do with the author's sen-

sibility and exuberant imagination. It is completely translatable. Once this comic approach entered into American
fiction, it altered the literature slightly and also enriched
it. In fact, in the craft of fiction writing, dramatic humor
is a major type of pleasure, its sources as inexhaustible as
human drama. Its realization depends on the capacity of
the individual author's talent. It is too pessimistic and too
narrow-minded to claim that nonnative speakers cannot
write playfully in English.

Nabokov had written extensively in Russian, and he
maintained that this was the essential difference between
himself and Conrad. Indeed, having written in Russian
could preempt most of his guilt about switching to English.
He wrote a number of novels and hundreds of poems in
Russian, and he spent ten years translating Pushkin's *Eugene
Onegin*. When the translation was done, he bantered that
Mother Russia should be grateful to him. Even so, he admitted that for him to write in English was a "private tragedy."
The tragedy is not that he might have written better in his
mother tongue but that he had to give the prime years of his
creative life to English, a language in which he never felt at
home. Furthermore, the brilliance of his English style may
be impossible to translate into Russian, or into any other
language. Yet despite the loss, he managed to pay tribute
to Russia and Russian literature, though he did so always
in his own manner and on his own terms. He is a supreme
example of how to adapt writing to the circumstances of
displacement, how to imagine and attain a place in the adopted language while still maintaining an intimate relationship with his mother tongue, and how to face an oppressive
regime with contempt, artistic integrity, and individual
dignity.

Still, there are writers, similar to Conrad, who have never had a chance to write in their native languages and are forced to choose another language. For them, the Nabokovian model may not be feasible, and they must find their own bearings and imagine their own places in the adopted languages while trying to form their unique relationships with their mother tongues. Ideally speaking, these writers should be able to contribute to the literatures of their original countries as well. But can this "dual loyalty" be possible? Is it not overreaching to expect so much of oneself? Indeed, it does seem an unreasonable goal. But most good writers are Don Quixote at heart, and unreasonableness is often a condition of art.

David Malouf, the Australian poet and novelist, wrote *The Imagined Life,* a novel based on the exile of Ovid, whose experiences in the wilderness far from Rome are unknown to us except for the glimpses of his sufferings revealed in his poems of exile. Ovid, as the narrator and the protagonist of the novel, reaches a kind of enlightenment toward the end of the story and returns to the wilderness with the boy he adopted. He imagines a language he would like to learn or recover: "When I think of my exile now it is from the universe. When I think of the tongue that has been taken away from me, it is some earlier and more universal language than our Latin, subtle as it undoubtedly is. Latin is a language for distinctions, every ending defines and divides. The language I am speaking of now, that I am almost speaking, is a language whose every syllable is a gesture of reconciliation. We knew that language once. I spoke it in my childhood. We must discover it again."[40] In the novel, Ovid did not elaborate more on this language, but we can see that it is a language of synthesis, based more on similarity than on difference. It is a language beyond mere signifiers.

For the creation of literature, a language of synthesis is necessary to make sure that one's work is more meaningful and more authentic. One principle of this language is translatability. In other words, if rendered into different languages, especially into the language spoken by the people the author writes about, the work still remains meaningful. In the postcolonial era, this literary principle also has ethical implications. Chinua Achebe, in his essay "An Image of Africa: Racism in Conrad's *Heart of Darkness*," speaks passionately and convincingly about the novella as a racist text, partly because Conrad did not treat the Africans as normal human beings in his story and instead depicted Africa as "the other world" existing outside human civilization. No matter how much one may like the novella, it does not speak to Africans. Imagine what kind of work it would become if the people it portrays could accept the story as literature that speaks also to them? The novella would grow into a masterpiece of universal significance and appeal.

I am aware that I may be simplifying the issue here. At some point, linguistic betrayal can be unavoidable if a writer adopts another language and wants to create a style largely based on wordplay. In such a case, should he comply with a neutral diction so as to produce the kind of "universal literature" that is entirely translatable as Amitav Ghosh describes in his essay "The March of the Novel through History"?[41] Or should he strive to create a style mainly bound to the adopted language, such as Nabokov's verbal feats? My answer is that he must do everything to find his place in his adopted language, including cracking jokes that are not translatable for his native people. In such a case, he may have to sacrifice his mother tongue, while borrowing its strength and resources, in order to accomplish a style in his adopted tongue. In short, he must be loyal only to his art.

On the other hand, even though the translation of a writer's work may lose some of its fun—especially in the case of word games—the meanings, the human experiences, and above all, the artistic spirit will survive and can resonate to other audiences if the work is genuine literature. I share Salman Rushdie's conviction "that something can be gained" in translation.[42] We ought to trust that talented translators can find ways to create playfulness that can compensate for some of what is lost. Therefore, the writer who adopts English, while striving to seek a place in this idiom, should also imagine ways to transcend any language.

An Individual's Homeland

Let me start with a well-known poem, "Ithaka," by the Greek poet C. P. Cavafy. The speaker of the poem talks about a journey, a lifelong one, and counsels his interlocutor on how to manage the trip psychologically:

> As you set out for Ithaka
> hope the voyage is a long one,
> full of adventure, full of discovery.
> Laistrygonians and Cyclops,
> angry Poseidon—don't be afraid of them:
> you'll never find things like that on your way
> as long as you keep your thoughts raised high,
> as long as a rare excitement
> stirs your spirit and your body.[1]

This poetic speech takes place in a situation where the listener is about to set out on a journey. The destination, as the poem's title designates, is "Ithaka," the city-state the ancient hero Odysseus headed toward on his way back from Troy. In Homer's epic, however, Ithaka, the kingdom Odysseus will regain, embodies losses to be recovered. It also stands for the promise of a heroic return.

In Cavafy's poem, however, the ancient meaning of Ithaka is changed—it is no longer the destination of a legendary warrior whose return is sponsored by deities; instead it has become an imagined end of a journey taken by a common man. Therefore, in the poem, Ithaka is a symbol of arrival, not of return. It represents what can be gained, not regained. In an allegorical sense, everyone should have his own Ithaka and travel toward it with "a rare excitement" and a constant vision, as the poem assures us: "Arriving there is what you are destined for," and once you have arrived, "you will have understood by then what these Ithakas mean." The plural form, "Ithakas," extenuates its epical connotations and multiplies the geographic image, which becomes pertinent to everyone, just as the "you" by now has also begun to refer to people in general, as well as the listener. At the same time, the beauty and subtlety of the word "Ithaka" resides in its mythological resonance, which evokes something in the past in the traveler's origin—something that has shaped his imagined destination. Although he finally reaches his Ithaka, his arrival cannot be completely separated from his point of departure, because his journey was effected by the vision of a legendary city whose historical and cultural significance constitutes part of his heritage. In thus defining the nature of the traveler's journey, we may reverse the beginning line of "East Coker" in T. S. Eliot's *Four Quartets* without violating its logic: In my end is my beginning.

★

Many exiles, emigrants, expatriates, and even some immigrants are possessed with the desire to someday return to their native lands. The nostalgia often deprives them of a sense of direction and prevents them from putting down roots anywhere. The present and the future have been impaired by their displacements, and their absence from their original countries gives them nothing but pain. American immigrant literature is full of characters like this, the majority of whom are men. Mr. Shimerda in *My Antonia*, after his Russian friends have left, shoots himself because he is lonely and cannot see the possibility settling down in the Nebraskan wilderness and because he misses his old life in Bohemia but cannot find a way to go back. Albert Schearl, the father in *Call It Sleep,* cannot stop missing life on his farm back in Europe, and as a result, he abandons his factory job and begins to deliver milk in New York—he prefers to drive a horse wagon, thinking he will be closer to his roots in farming. Albert buys a pair of bull's horns and happily shows them to his wife Genya. The horns represent his former life, his sexual prowess, and also his guilty past in which he saw a crazed bull goring his father to death but didn't help the old man. Albert's nostalgia has dulled his memory and kept him from seeing the full symbolic meaning of the bull's horns. Consequently, the horns turn destructive later in the story, bearing witness to the dark secret of his past. Carlos Chang, the father in Sigrid Nunez's novel *A Feather on the Breath of God* (1995), is another man destroyed by nostalgia. Chang is half Chinese and half Panamanian and always misses China, where he spent less than ten years in his childhood. All his close Chinese relatives were killed by the Japanese, and the China he remembers is already gone. Still, he cannot leave that place mentally, continues to wait tables in Chinatown, and even isolates himself from his daughters who were raised by his wife as Germans. Nostalgia robs him of the ability to move elsewhere, and he falls through the gaps between different cultures and languages in America. We don't know if he is even literate in any language; it is likely he cannot read. Similarly, his wife Christa, a German bride he brought to the United States, never stops dreaming of going back to Germany. But once she goes back to visit, she realizes that Germany is no longer the same place. Still, she never finds a proper place in her adopted country. In Nunez's novel, ironically but quite significantly, the violent Vadim, a recent Russian immigrant, manages to survive and even thrive in New York mainly because he accepts the fact that he cannot go back to his native land anymore and has to make good here, though he too is afflicted with nostalgia.

Opposite to nostalgia is the longing to go somewhere, to leave the old place and settle down in a new place, or to be on the move constantly. Bertha, a new immigrant in *Call It Sleep,* would never go back to Austria, though she would send money to her parents. To her, the home village is a lifeless place, a place she is glad to have "escaped" from. Therefore, she declares proudly that she "doesn't yearn for the homeland." In Joyce's *A Portrait of an Artist as a Young Man,* Stephen Dedalus has to leave Ireland to grow into an artist so that he can, as he claims, "encounter for the millionth time the reality of experience and to forge in the smithy of [his] soul the uncreated conscience of [his] race." In addition to "exile," he carries two other weapons for self-protection, namely, "silence" and "cunning." By "silence," he means to let his work speak for him, whereas "cunning" implies that he would model himself after the archetypical exile Odysseus,[2] who is often called "the cunning one" or "the resourceful man" in Homer's epic and who gains his name mainly through his wanderings.

In our postcolonial era, displacement also takes a new form—many people from formerly colonized countries move to the West as refugees or immigrants. In some cases, their homelands no longer exist, and they have no choice but to look for home elsewhere. By definition, the word "homeland" has two meanings—one meaning refers to one's native land, and the other to the land where one's home is at present. In the past, the two meanings were easy to reconcile because "home" also signified "origin" and the past and the present were inseparable. In our time, however, the two meanings tend to form a dichotomy. Thus, we hear the expressions "my new homeland," "my second homeland," "my newly adopted homeland," or "homeland security." We may come across lines like these: "My mother always said / your homeland is any place, / preferably the place where you die."[3] In other words, homeland is no longer a place that exists in one's past but a place also relevant to one's present and future.

Conventionally, a person's homeland is his country of origin, to which he longs to return no matter where he goes. A Chinese proverb summarizes this longing: "Gold nests and silver nests, none is as nice as your own straw nest." In addition to nostalgia, there is also our innate but unreasonable belief that success means much more if it is appreciated by the people of one's native land. In Samuel Johnson's words, "Every man has a lurking wish to appear considerable in his native place." Again, the Chinese language has a peculiar expression for this hankering: "Return home robed in silk and brocade and glorify your ancestors." But if we examine these sentiments carefully in literary contexts, we can find that even traditional literature does not always subscribe to them.

The most celebrated return in classical literature is Odysseus's return to Ithaka, where he kills the surly suitors of his wife Penelope, restores his household, and reclaims his kingship. Yet his homecoming does not turn out to be as triumphant as he envisioned. While in exile, he imagines his homeland as the sweetest place on earth, as he tells Lord Alcinous, his host on Scherie Island: "Ithaka . . . lies slanting to the west. . . . It is a rough land, but a fit nurse for men. And I, for one, know of no sweeter sight for a man's eyes than his own country. . . . So true it is that his motherland and his parents are what a man holds sweetest, even though he may have settled far away from his people in some rich home in foreign lands."[4] Though platitudinous, these words are sincerely spoken and express the hero's deep love and longing for his homeland. However, later when Odysseus actually lands on the shore of Ithaka, something extraordinary happens: "everything in Ithaka, the long hillpaths, the quiet bays, the beetling rocks, and the green trees seemed unfamiliar to its King. He leapt to his feet and stood staring at his native land. Then he groaned, and slapping his thighs with the flat of his hands gave vent to his disappointment: 'Alas! Whose country have I come to now? Are they some brutal tribe of lawless savages, or a kindly and godfearing people? Where shall I put all these goods of mine, and where on earth am I myself to go?'"[5] As if a stranger, Odysseus fails to recognize his own homeland. His confusion originates from two facts: first, in his twenty years of exile, he has changed and so has his memory of his homeland; second, his homeland has also changed, no longer matching his memory of it. This episode illuminates the truth of the relationship between oneself and one's native land after a long absence from it—one cannot return to the same place as the same person.

In another surprising turn of events in the *Odyssey,* after regaining his kingdom, Odysseus does not stay in Ithaka to grow into his dotage. It is revealed that he will have to embark on another adventure. In "The Book of the Dead," Odysseus visits the Underground where he encounters numerous ghosts. The prophet Tiresias is among them, and he discloses the future to Odysseus:

> It is true that you will pay out these men for their misdeeds when you reach home. But whichever way you choose to kill them, whether by stratagem or in a straight fight with the naked sword, when you have cleared your palace of these Suitors, you must then set out once more upon your travels. You must take a well-cut oar and go on till you reach a people who know nothing of the sea and never use salt with their food, so that our crimson-painted ships and the long oars that serve those ships as wings are quite beyond their ken. And this will be your cue—a very clear one, which you cannot miss. When you fall in with some other traveller who speaks of the "winnowing-fan" you are carrying on your shoulder, the time will have come for you to plant your shapely oar in the earth and offer Lord Poseidon the rich sacrifice of a ram, a bull, and a breeding-boar. Then go back home and make ceremonial offerings to the immortal gods who live in the broad heavens, to all of them, this time, in due precedence. As for your own end, Death will come to you out of the sea, Death in his gentlest guise. When he takes you, you will be worn out after an easy old age surrounded by a prosperous people.[6]

Later in book 23, when he and Penelope are finally reunited, Odysseus repeats Tiresias's prophecy and makes it clear to her that he will have to go through one more ordeal and that he doesn't know how long the ordeal will last (11, 263–84). His desire for adventure is so earnest that he must tell her this at the very moment she recognizes him. This wanderlust suggests that his restored home is no longer a place where he will feel at peace.

Tiresias's prophecy is a seminal episode in literature, which Dante later transformed in his *Inferno*. Odysseus— who, contrary to Tiresias's prediction, did not die peacefully at home—appears in the Eighth Circle of Hell to greet Dante and Virgil and describes to them another adventure he had: a maritime one instead of, or in addition to, the landlocked journey foretold by Tiresias. In Ithaka, Odysseus gathered a small band of his remaining men, who had also managed to come home and who were now old and slow, and persuaded them to set sail with him for the uncharted seas. He was inevitably restless at home, as if unhinged by Circe and Calypso, with whom he had stayed as a lover for one and seven years, respectively—fathering and leaving behind three sons on their distant islands. Indeed, the former exile seemed afflicted with an illness, avaricious for adventure and knowledge. The eloquence of his oratory stirred his men to leave their homeland with him again:

> "O brothers who have reached the west," I began,
> "Through a hundred thousand perils, surviving all:
>
> So little is the vigil we see remain
> Still for our senses, that you should not choose
> To deny it the experience—behind the sun

Leading us onward—of the world which has

No people in it. Consider well your seed:

You were not born to live as a mere brute does,

But for the pursuit of knowledge and the good."[7]

Although Odysseus sounds noble and convincing here, Dante actually presents him as a sinner giving fraudulent counsel that leads his men to the bottom of the sea together with himself. Besides the deception, Odysseus also flouted the classical ethos of *pietes* (dutifulness)—putting aside his love for his wife and son and renouncing his responsibilities as the king.[8] In other words, in pursuit of truth and self-fulfillment, he forsook his homeland, along with all his attachments, and became self-centered. Dante calls Odysseus's journey a "mad adventure" (*Paradiso*, XXVII: 82); probably it reminded him of his own exile, an experience that can easily drive the individual to take an extreme course of action in fulfilling his talent and manifesting his pride.

Alfred Tennyson picked up on this episode from Dante and gave it another treatment in his poem "Ulysses," a dramatic monologue spoken by Odysseus. The poem suppresses Dante's negative perspective on Odysseus's final journey and instead celebrates his audacity to challenge the boundary of human experience and knowledge. Tennyson himself stated that the poem "Ulysses" expressed his own "need of going forward and braving the struggle of life" after the death of his friend Arthur Hallam.[9] In the poem, Odysseus, though aged, is stronger in will and spirit and more eloquent in his speech. He declares:

> Yet all experience is an arch wherethrough
> Gleams that untraveled world whose margin fades
> Forever and forever when I move.
> How dull it is to pause, to make an end,
> To rust unburnished, not to shine in use. (19–23)

The desire for adventure and knowledge compels Odysseus to leave his scepter and the kingdom of Ithaka to his son Telemachus. If he set out by himself like an exile addicted to wandering, the journey could be easier to justify, because the perils and the sacrifice would involve only himself and his family and he would not put other lives in danger. But he misleads a whole group of grizzled men into a suicidal situation. As they are embarking, Odysseus commands his followers this way:

> Come, my friends,
> 'Tis not too late to seek a newer world.
> Push off, and sitting well in order smite
> The sounding furrows; for my purpose holds
> To sail beyond the sunset, and the baths
> Of all the western stars, until I die. (56–61)

The great orator has dropped his disguise and bluntly admits his own "purpose" to be the motivation of the journey; he also makes it clear that this is their last adventure together as he is explicit about the duration of the trip: "until I die." In eulogizing Odysseus as the ultimate spirit of human quest for truth and knowledge, Tennyson did not, or could not, suppress the fatal flaw in his hero, who has become egoistic and destructive to others because he is not bound by his duty to his past, his family, and his homeland.

More dreadful is that Odysseus here confuses his personal longing with the collective needs and, as a result, brings the whole crew to their deaths. He does this with clear awareness of the outcome but without regard to the cost of the others' lives. In this sense, he is more awful, if not more insane, than the Odysseus in *Inferno*.

We often talk about exile and solitude as two modes of existence that are not only inseparable but also intensify each other. What the episodes from Dante and Tennyson suggest is that exile must be an individual, private experience that is so personal that solitude ought to be its ethical condition.

Odysseus's return (and its sequel) is still invoked by writers today. Milan Kundera's *Ignorance* portrays the experience of contemporary emigrations with this classical episode as a backdrop. Meditating on Odysseus's return, the narrator of the novel reasons, "Rather than ardent exploration of the unknown (adventure), he chose the apotheosis of the known (return). Rather than the infinite (for adventure never intends to finish), he chose the finite (for the return is a reconciliation with the finitude of life)."[10] Then, the narrator turns to the moment when Odysseus was left by the Phaeacian seamen on the shore of Ithaka but failed to realize where he was. In fact, for its thematic depth, the whole novel—about Irena's and Josef's returns to their native Czechoslovakia after the collapse of the Soviet Union and after their long stays in the West—hinges on the Homeric episode that shows the homeland as an alien place to the returned exiles. According to Kundera, Homer "glorified nostalgia," which to the novelist means "suffering" intensified by "ignorance," or "something like the pain of ignorance"; Kundera points out that the Greek word *nostos* (return) and the Latin word *ignorare* (to be unaware of; to miss or lack) both have contributed to the formation of the meanings of the word "nostalgia" in various European languages (ibid., 5–7). His understanding of the sinister nature of nostalgia is so profound that he believes nostalgia actually impairs one's memory, as if there is an inverse ratio between memory and nostalgia—the stronger one's nostalgia is, the less one can remember. Kundera also applies this principle to the Greek hero's situation: "During the twenty years of Odysseus's absence, the people of Ithaca retained many recollections of him but never felt nostalgia for him" (ibid., 33). Indeed, nostalgia is never a collective emotion and is merely the exiled individual's one-sided wish. In the novel, Odysseus, once home, realizes that the essence of his life lies elsewhere—in the twenty years of his wanderings. Similar to the ancient hero, neither Irena nor Josef can find home again in their native land. Their returns are failures because they don't have a homeland anymore. In their countrymen's eyes, they are foreigners; for a long time, they did not exist to their countrymen at all, not until their sudden reappearances. After this painful return, Irena will probably become a migrant between Paris and Prague, whereas Josef heads back to the home he used to share with his late wife in Denmark, a country where he has never felt at home.

In the present era, airplanes and the Internet can keep us close in touch with our native lands. The issue of return is no longer physical, but it is an issue of how we view our past and whether we accept it as part of ourselves. In *Ignorance*, Kundera does not deal with this subject directly, but he dramatizes it through describing the power of the mother tongue over the exiles. Although Josef finds that the Czech language has changed considerably—at first it's almost incomprehensible to him, but after three days in Czechoslovakia, he experiences the thrill of speaking it fluently again. "Now . . . the words leaped from his mouth on their own, without his having to hunt for them, monitor them" (ibid., 157). This never happens when he speaks Danish, in which he always hesitates and stumbles. Later, in his sexual encounter with Irena toward the end of the novel, both of them speak their mother tongue, which at once unleashes the energy of their common past. This climatic scene is laced with meanings:

How unexpected! How intoxicating! For the first time in twenty years, he hears those dirty Czech words and instantly he is aroused to a degree he has never been since he left his country, because all those words—coarse, dirty, obscene— only have power over him in his native language (in the language of Ithaca), since it is through that language, through its deep roots, that the arousal of generations and generations surges up in him. Until this moment these two have not even kissed. And now thrillingly, magnificently aroused, in a matter of seconds they begin to make love.

Their accord is total, for she too is aroused by the words she has neither said nor heard for so many years. A total accord in an explosion of obscenities! Ah, how impoverished her life has been! All the vices missed out on, all the infidelities left unrealized—all of that she is avid to experience. (Ibid., 178–79)

In their native land, the only thing that is meaningful to both of them and that is able to bind them together is their mother tongue, which is their true heritage and which in fact they do not have to return to Prague to speak. Wherever they go, their mother tongue will remain relatively intact within them. In the context of the novel, this is a moment of revelation: they find that their real homeland actually exists within their own beings. Language, sexuality, and heritage are entangled here, but none of them is bound to a specific place for its existence and manifestation. What is needed is a shared space in which the two individuals can interact and communicate intimately. To put this in a matter-of-fact way, to the two lovers, a hotel bed is more essential than a city or a country. Symbolically, the emigrants' need for their native land is called into question.

A more sensible question in this regard should be how to deal with one's past, which also encompasses one's native country. In contemporary fiction, no novel, to my knowledge, addresses the issue of the past more radically than V. S. Naipaul's *A Bend in the River,* a book very close to my heart. One of the themes of the novel is the search for home—all its main characters have no homeland to speak of, and even the white man Raymond has to seek employment and find home outside his native Europe. The narrator and protagonist, Salim, explains why he left home for the interior of Africa: "I could no longer submit to Fate. My wish was not to be good, in the way of our tradition, but to make good. But how? What did I have to offer? What talent, what skill, apart from the African trading skills of our family? This anxiety began to eat away at me."[11] To Salim, "to make good" means to make the best of the hopeless situation in which his clan is forced to disintegrate and in which their traditional values can no longer hold things together. It also means he has to leave home and find his own way of surviving. Indeed, for him, as for all the main characters of the novel, there is no homeland as recourse. Faith or loyalty (to whom and to what?) is cheap and meaningless to a struggling individual like Salim, though his old friend Nazruddin believes he is "the most faithful man."

The phrase "trample on the past" recurs throughout the book like a refrain, and each time it deepens and complicates the message. It is Indar, the African-Indian educated in England, who first voices the notion. When he has come back to Africa to teach at the polytechnic, he tells Salim: "'You stop grieving for the past. You see that the past is something in your mind alone, that it doesn't exist in real life. You trample on the past, you crush it. In the beginning it is like trampling on a garden. In the end you are just walking on ground. That is the way we have to learn to live now. The past is here.' He touched his heart. 'It isn't there.' And he pointed at the dusty road" (ibid., 112–13). We can see the contradiction in Indar's startling discourse: if the past does not exist—if it is a nonentity—then how can one crush it like trampling on a garden? What Indar really means is that the past has no meaning as a sentiment and that it is merely extra baggage that hinders one's survival. By this logic, if the past is not useful at all, one should get rid of it.

Intelligent and perceptive as Indar is, he cannot help but act like most people and search for recourse to his past—even though it may amount to reaching out for his family's Indian origin. After graduating from a famous university in England, he cannot find a job, even though his schoolmates can, and he does not receive any of the brown envelopes from the hiring companies that the other graduates get regularly. At the suggestion of a woman lecturer, he goes to the Indian Embassy in London in hopes of becoming a diplomat, selling himself as "an extraordinary man, a man of two worlds." Once inside the embassy, he is like a ball tossed back and forth by the bureaucrats, and finally, one of them

condescends to speak to him, "But you say in your letter you
are from Africa. How can you join our diplomatic service?
How can we have a man of divided loyalties?" (ibid., 149).
The shock brings Indar back to his true condition, a man
without a country and without an identity—even his man-
hood is somewhat throttled. This realization makes him
more assertive, as he discloses his state of mind to Salim:

> I belonged to myself alone. I was going to surrender my
> manhood to nobody. For someone like me there was only
> one civilization and one place—London, or a place like it.
> Every other kind of life was make-believe. Home—what for?
> To hide? To bow to our great men? For people in our situ-
> ation, people led into slavery, that is the biggest trap of all.
> We have nothing. We solace ourselves with the idea of the
> great men of our tribe, the Gandhi and the Nehru, and we
> castrate ourselves. "Here take my manhood and invest it for
> me. Take my manhood and be a greater man yourself, for my
> sake!" No! I want to be a man myself. (Ibid., 151–52)

The last sentence—"I want to be a man myself"—is a desperate cry for Indar's own existence, and it echoes every
man's struggle for self-fulfillment. It raises a universal and
perennial question—how to realize one's selfhood under
the shadow of the great men of one's tribe? In our time, the
answer to this question often precludes the necessity of the
past if the past means nothing but servitude.

   To understand this principle is one thing, and to live by it
is another. Unlike Salim, Indar always acts like a man from
a wealthy family, though he is not rich. In other words, his
life is overshadowed by his once-affluent family. Try as he
might, he cannot find his place in London or in the United

States and is finally content with a job below his caliber. He grows softheaded and sentimental, dreaming of a small village he might return to. Salim concludes: "The younger Indar was wiser. Use the airplane; trample on the past, as Indar had said he had trampled on the past. Get rid of that idea of the past; make the dream-like scenes of the loss ordinary" (ibid., 244). Unlike Indar, Salim puts into practice the principle of trampling on the past. He goes deep into Africa, to the town at a bend of the big river, to escape from the tides of historical violence that will break and swallow his clan. When the town on the river is ruled by political terror, he sets out for England to join his fiancée-to-be, Kareisha. For him, as well as for his friend Nazruddin, the way of survival is to always move a step ahead of the destructive force, and for that reason, they have to flee from their past constantly. That they both end up in London is a historical irony—they can find home, impermanent though it is, only in the center of the old colonial power.

Yet if we look at Salim's case closely, we can see that he has not shed his past as completely as he claims. But rather, he manages to utilize it without letting it overburden him. In the novel, the past no longer takes the form of a place or an ethnic group, but that of one's cultural and familial heritage, which is impossible to wipe out no matter how hard one tramples on it. There is a crucial detail in the story that Naipaul downplayed considerably; that is, Salim holds a British passport. This is not just proof of his identity as a colonial but also a privilege that enables him to travel, especially to the West. Unlike Salim, his servant Metty does not have such a privilege and is trapped in the town. He begs Salim to take him away, but his patron replies, "how can I take you with me, Metty? The world isn't like that nowadays.

There are visas and passports. I can hardly arrange these things for myself. I don't know where I'm going or what I'll do. I hardly have any money. I'm scarcely able to look after myself" (ibid., 274–75). This is the only moment the story discloses the importance of Salim's passport. Compared with Metty, Salim is actually empowered by his colonial past, which is embodied by the papers that would enable him to escape. Not as sharp as Salim, Metty has mistakenly returned to his African origin by joining Salim in the town, and for some time, he thrives and is liked by local women, but when things turn bad, the locals begin to view him as an outsider. Theotime, the appropriator of Salim's shop, even treats Metty as a slave. Metty's predicament is an example of one's native land having deteriorated into a nightmarish quagmire.

Another aspect of the past Salim has never dropped is his friendship with Nazruddin, to whose daughter he will be engaged eventually. Through Nazruddin, Salim starts his business in the African town with an eye toward getting in touch with European civilization there and toward becoming a man like Nazruddin. Also, through the older man, Salim eventually arrives in London. His claim of having destroyed his past is at most partially true. As a man without a homeland, he accepts migration as his existential condition and fixes his mind on arrival, and at the same time, he makes the best use of his past after jettisoning a good part of it.

For many migrant writers, homeland is actually their mother tongues, as the German poet Hilde Domin states, "For me language is impossible to lose, after everything else has been lost. The last, essential home."[12] However, this home is also a kind of privilege that not every writer can have. To live and work in one's mother tongue, the migrant writer must root his existence in the language. If he does not use it frequently, his mother tongue will shrink and gradually lose its freshness, suffering from a "linguistic lag" from the current idiom spoken back in his native land. If he is a poet, he may strive to preserve the purity of his mother tongue by using a literary language relatively detached from the current idiom. He may even add some nuances to his poetic language because he sees his mother tongue in the context of other languages now. But if he is a fiction writer, he will need to keep up with the ever-changing speech of his mother tongue, unless his subject matter is not contemporary. The ideal situation is to have a job where he uses his native language every day, such as teaching the language and literature as Czeslaw Milosz did at Berkeley, or, less advantageously, writing for newspapers as Isaac Bashevis Singer did for the Yiddish daily *Forward*. In addition, the migrant writer should be able to live among the native speakers of his mother tongue from time to time, as some Chinese writers living in North America return to China annually to "recharge themselves." But some migrant writers do not have any of those opportunities and have to make a living outside their mother tongues. Furthermore, there is the problem of audience. Some writers already have an audience in their mother tongues, which can serve as a haven wherein they continue to prove their existence (yet this is not always a blessing; for example, Isaac Bashevis Singer often thought of committing suicide because of the demise of Yiddish), whereas other writers have no audience in their mother tongues and have to work in the language of the adopted country. To the latter writers, the mother tongue is an unavailable "home"—their survival depends more or less on estrangement from the mother tongue, and their ambition may lie in another language in which they have to figure out how to survive.

I am not prescribing a formula for migrant writers here, because everyone has his own way of becoming a writer. The underlying principle is how to survive as an artist while making one's art thrive.

The German writer W. G. Sebald presents a model of artistic survival in his book *The Emigrants*. The book consists of four narratives, told by the same narrator, about four dislocated and traumatized men, Dr. Henry Selwyn, Paul Bereyter, Ambros Adelwarth, and Max Ferber. Three of them are Jews who escaped the Holocaust but suffered inner damage. These four displaced protagonists are not only victims of depression but are also crippled emotionally. None of them has children, as if their displacements sterilized them. For decades, especially in their prime years, they have all tried suppressing their memories of the past, which will catch and overpower them when they are no longer physically and mentally strong. Three of them commit suicide, overtaken by the dark forces of the past. However, unlike the three suicidal men, Max Ferber—modeled on the English Jewish painter Frank Auerbach—survives and eventually grows into a significant artist. Why is he not destroyed by the memories of the past? How does he manage to survive and to do his work? What does he do that is conducive to his sanity and artistic growth? These questions are the key to understanding the book, which, besides narrating the tragic stories of human folly, also teaches the wisdom of survival.

Miraculously, at every opportunity, Max Ferber makes the right choice consciously or unconsciously, which helps him construct an integral space in which he can live and

work. Like the other three protagonists, Ferber also sup-
pressed his memories of the painful past. When he was a
young boy, his parents, though unable to flee Germany
themselves, sent him to England to study in a private
school. He had no idea about the violence unleashed on the
Jews back in Germany and viewed his correspondence with
his parents as a chore. When his parents were rounded up
for the concentration camp and their letters stopped com-
ing, he felt relieved. From then on, he would never speak his
mother tongue again—to him, it would mean nothing but
pain and horror. This automatic suppression of his mother
tongue is essential for his survival. Eventually, German fades
in his mind to a mere "echo, a muted and incomprehensible
murmur."[13] Yet unlike the other three protagonists, Ferber
later does find the nerve to grasp the pain of his past, as he
goes to Colmar to look at the Grunewald paintings, which
both unnerve him and provide insights into the nature of
pain. He tells the narrator, presumably Sebald, "I gradually
understood that, beyond a certain point, pain blots out the
one thing that is essential to its being experienced—consciousness—and so perhaps extinguishes itself" (ibid., 170).
For all those years, he didn't feel the pain of loss because it
was so intense it became "painless" to him. This is also the
emotional state in which the other suicidal men enclosed
themselves. With the new understanding, Ferber goes on to
Lake Geneva to retrace the old memories he dared not disturb before. For the first time, he carefully reads the memoir
his mother wrote before she was shipped to the concentration camp, and later, he hands the memoir to Sebald as a
testimonial to the loss and destruction the Jews suffered.
Through confronting the painful past, Ferber finally can accept it as part of his being.

Despite his apparent modesty, Ferber is a great artist in spirit. This spiritual aspect was conspicuous even when he was a teenager. At the age of eighteen, he studied in Manchester and lodged at 104 Palatine Road, in the same brick house where the philosopher Ludwig Wittgenstein had once lived as a young engineering student. This coincidence instilled in Ferber the sentiment that he was connected with the great man, and thus a spiritual bond was established between himself and those before him. The narrator relates, "Doubtless any retrospective connection with Wittgenstein was purely illusory, but it meant no less to him on that account, said Ferber. Indeed, he sometimes felt as if he were tightening his ties to those who had gone before; . . . he was aware of a sense of brotherhood that reached far back beyond his own lifetime or even the years immediately before it" (ibid., 166–67). To put this more explicitly, he feels he belongs among the great, and this sentiment sustains him spiritually. My point can be verified by another detail that appears later in the narrative. Two decades after Sebald left Manchester, when he meets with Ferber again in his studio in 1989, Ferber greets him like this, "Aren't we all getting on! He said it with a throwaway smile, and then, not seeming to me to have aged in the slightest, gestured toward a copy of Rembrandt's portrait of a man with a magnifying glass, which still hung in the same place on the wall as it had twenty-five years before, and added: Only he doesn't seem to get any older" (ibid., 180). Clearly, Ferber has kept Rembrandt as a member of his spiritual community, and the position of the master's work in his studio has never been disturbed. This presence of the great spirit forms the center of Ferber's working space—also, the center of his consciousness.

On the other hand, there is a profound sense of loneliness, hopelessness, and humility in the character of Max Ferber, and he shows the qualities of a genuine artist. For decades, he has painted ten hours a day, seven days a week, without any glimmer of success. He feels that he is getting nowhere and has failed completely. His studio is covered with dust that he will not disturb as he prefers dust to air, light, and water. The narrator describes his workplace as follows:

Since he applied the paint thickly, and then repeatedly scratched it off the canvas as his work proceeded, the floor was covered with a largely hardened and encrusted deposit of droppings, mixed with coal dust, several centimetres thick at the centre and thinning out towards the outer edges, in places resembling the flow of lava. This, said Ferber, was the true product of his continuing endeavours and the most palpable proof of his failure. (Ibid., 161)

The daily practice of his art is no more than an accumulation of dust. Such a hopeless outlook verges on despair. Even Sebald never thought Ferber would become a significant painter. Ferber paints every day just as a way to spend his life, like Kafka's hunger artist who fasts because he cannot find another way to exist and his fasting eventually grows meaningless to everyone, even to himself.

However, Ferber is not an artist of art for art's sake. He is aware of his social existence, which is also part of the frame of reference he has constructed for himself. In May 1945, at the age of twenty, after he had recuperated from his jaundice and had been released from the hospital, he walked forty-five miles to Manchester, an industrial city clouded with coal dust at the time, to resume his art studies. Originally, he went there to avoid joining his uncle in New York so as to disentangle himself from his past, but the gloomy city took hold of him once he arrived, and he felt he "had found his destiny." He felt he could not move anywhere else for the rest of his life, nor did he want to move. Manchester was an immigrant city, according to him, and full of Jews, including many German Jews; throughout Europe, said the narrator, no city had a stronger German Jewish influence than Manchester. As a result, Ferber has actually lived in his past. He confesses, "although I had intended to move in the opposite direction, when I arrived in Manchester I had come home, in a sense, and . . . I am here . . . to serve under the chimney" (ibid., 191–92). Unlike the protagonists of the other three narratives in *Emigrants,* Ferber alone has kept an appropriate relationship with his past. He accepts it as part of the quotidian reality and has managed to live with it while maintaining some artistic detachment from it. It is the intimate and inseverable connection with his past that keeps him sane and safe and provides for him the space in which he can practice his art. In other words, he has succeeded in constructing a kind of homeland for himself, to survive the violence and horror of history.

Obviously, in the literary examples I have discussed above, we can see that for most migrants, especially migrant artists and writers, the issue of homeland involves arrival more than return. The dichotomy inherent in the word "homeland" is more significant now than it was in the past. Its meaning can no longer be separated from home, which is something the migrant should be able to build away from his native land. Therefore, it is logical to say that your homeland is where you build your home.

The Norwegian American writer O. E. Rolvaag wrote his epic novel *Giants in the Earth* in 1924. When he had finished the book about the Norwegian settlers' struggle on the Dakota plains, he said, "Fifty years from now this work ... should have greater significance than it does now."[14] Now, more than eighty years later, the novel still speaks to us. There is a moving scene toward the end of the novel, in which the minister decides to return to the makeshift church (literally the protagonist Per Hansa Holm's sod house) to conduct Communion services. The altar of the "church" is to be the big immigrant chest the Holms hauled all the way from Norway.[15] This use of the chest as the foundation of the church symbolizes that the immigrants, though afflicted with homesickness and fear, have at last found their homeland in the prairie. Before the arrival of the minister, Per Hansa's wife Beret made her husband promise to bury her in the chest that used to belong to her father, should she die in the wilderness. The establishment of the church finally convinces her of the possibility of founding a civilization on the vast, unpopulated land.[16] This classic scene in American literature illustrates the appropriate use of the past in establishing the immigrants' present existential order.

Let me again invoke Cavafy's poem "Ithaka." Since most of us cannot go home again, we have to look for our own Ithakas and try to find ways to get there. Indeed, some of the Ithakas may turn out to be different from what we expected, but with such destinations in mind, we can have wonderful journeys that will enrich and enlighten us. Such a vision of arrival is, in fact, very American, especially in the immigrant experience, as most immigrants have come to America with the knowledge that to return to their land of origin will be unlikely. However, we should also bear in mind that, no matter where we go, we cannot shed our past completely—so we must strive to use parts of our past to facilitate our journeys. As we travel along, we should also imagine how to rearrange the landscapes of our envisioned homelands.

Notes

THE SPOKESMAN AND THE TRIBE

1. Quoted in Joseph Pearce, *Solzhenitsyn: A Soul in Exile* (Grand Rapids, Mich.: Baker Books, 2001), 228.

2. Ibid., 231.

3. D. M. Thomas, *Alexander Solzhenitsyn: A Century in His Life* (New York: St. Martin's, 1998), 458.

4. Ibid., 468 and 475.

5. Pearce, *Solzhenitsyn*, 279.

6. Ibid., 274 and 282.

7. Sten Lee Meyers, "Solzhenitsyn Returns, on Russian TV," *New York Times,* February 9, 2006.

8. Dudley Clendinen, "Solzhenitsyn Secluded as Wife Becomes a Citizen," *New York Times,* June 25, 1985.

9. Pearce, *Solzhenitsyn*, 254.

10. For example, in *Cancer Ward,* Oleg, after his release from the ward, went to the zoo, observed a spiral-horn goat for a long time, and was moved by it. "Oleg stood there for five minutes and departed in admiration. The goat had not even stirred. That was the sort of character a man needed to get through life." *Cancer Ward,* trans.

Nicholas Bethell and David Burg (New York: Bantam, 1969), 503. In *The First Circle,* Innokenty tells his sister-in-law's husband, Galakhov, who is a famous but not significant writer, "And a great writer—forgive me, perhaps I shouldn't say this, I'll lower my voice—a great writer is, so to speak, a second government. That's why no regime anywhere has ever loved its great writers, only its minor ones." *The First Circle,* trans. Thomas P. Whitney (New York: Bantam Books, 1969), 415.

11. Some Russians still found Solzhenitsyn's "Americanness" problematic, even though he remained a Russian citizen. At a town meeting, one of the attendees rebuked Solzhenitsyn, "It is you and your writing that started it all and brought our country to the verge of collapse and devastation. Russia doesn't need you. So . . . go back to your blessed America." Quoted by Edward E. Ericson, Jr., in "Introduction to the Perennial Classics Edition," *The Gulag Archipelago (1918–1956)* (New York: Perennial Classics, 2002), xv.

12. Thomas, *Alexander Solzhenitsyn,* 458 and 467.

13. Quoted in Pearce, *Solzhenitsyn,* 282 and 249.

14. Yutang Lin, *My Country and My People* (New York: John Day, 1935), 100–108.

15. Ibid., 101.

16. Lin once explained, "Many people have advised me to get naturalized, but I've told them here is not a place to settle down, so we would rent rather than buy a home." Quoted by Xiping Wan, *On Lin Yutang* (Xian: Shanxi People's Press, 1987), 46.

17. Taiyi Lin, *Biography of Lin Yutang* (Taipei: Lianjing Publishing, 1990), 203.

18. Quoted in Zeng Jijin, "Standing at the Crossroads of Eastern and Western Cultures," *Chinese Writers,* no. 4 (2006), 109.

19. Lin Yutang, *My Country and My People* (New York: John Day, 1935), 15.

20. Pearl Buck, "Introduction," in ibid., xii.

21. *Lin Yutang Quanji* [Collected works by Ling Yutang] (Jilin: Dongbei Teachers University Press, 1994), 10:314.

22. See *Moment in Peking* (New York: John Day, 1939), 53–54, 96–97, and 257.

23. Taiyi Lin, *Biography of Lin Yutang,* 242.

24. Pearce, *Solzhenitsyn,* 260–61.

25. Salman Rushide, *Shame* (New York: Knopf, 1983), 90.

26. Ibid., 92.

27. V. S. Naipaul, *The Enigma of Arrival* (New York: Knopf, 1987), 98–99.

28. V. S. Naipaul, *Between Father and Son: Family Letters* (New York: Knopf, 2000), 283.

29. Ibid., 277.

30. In the late 1920s and early 1930s, Lin Yutang was nicknamed "King of Royalties," and his income from his writings surpassed any individual author's in China.

31. V. S. Naipaul, *A Bend in the River* (New York: Vintage, 1989), 85.

32. Ha Jin, *Facing Shadows* (New York: Hanging Loose Press, 1996), 62.

33. V. S. Naipaul, *Literary Occasions* (New York: Vintage, 2003), 181–82.

34. Nadine Grodimer, *The Essential Gesture: Writing, Politics, and Places*, ed. Stephen Clingman (New York: Knopf, 1988), 290.

35. Derek Walcott, *Collected Poems* (New York: Farrar, Straus, 1986), 346.

36. Andrei Makine, *Dreams of My Russian Summers*, trans. Geoffrey Strachan (New York: Scribner, 1997), 238.

THE LANGUAGE OF BETRAYAL

1. Milan Kundera, *Ignorance*, trans. Linda Asher (New York: HarperCollins, 2003), 8.

2. Joseph Brodsky, *Less than One: Selected Essays* (New York: Penguin, 1986), 357.

3. Vladimir Nabokov, *Strong Opinions* (New York: MaGraw-Hill, 1973), 113.

4. In fact, at the time Conrad had Russian citizenship, which his relatives tried repeatedly to help him get out of, but all the efforts came to nothing. See Zdzistaw Najder, *Joseph Conrad: A Chronicle* (New Brunswick, N.J.: Rutgers University Press, 1983), 33.

5. Quoted in Jeffrey Meyers, *Joseph Conrad: A Biography* (London: John Murray, 1991), 355. Frederick R. Karl, in *Joseph Conrad: Three Lives* (New York: Farrar, Straus, 1979), describes Conrad's repeated efforts to catch the attention of the Nobel Prize Committee since 1919 while at the same time turning down all honors offered by individual nations. Karl writes, "Conrad did not wish his name put forward for the Order of Merit, since he did not feel it was appropriate

for one who could not 'claim English literature as my literature' to receive such an honor. The Nobel Prize, however, was an international award and 'less in the nature of an honor than of mere reward, [and] we needn't have any scruples about acceptance if it ever comes in our way'" (822–23).

6. Quoted in Adam Gillon, "Words beyond the Life of Ships: Joseph Conrad's Impact on Polish Poetry," *Conradiana,* Spring–Summer 2002, 133–34. Gillon's essay gives a full account of the poetic reception of Conrad in Poland, and it concludes with this sentence: "Nowhere is Conrad as popular as in the country he had left."

7. Quoted in Ludwik Krzyzanowski, "Joseph Conrad: Some Polish Documents," *Joseph Conrad: Centennial Essays,* ed. Ludwik Kryzanowski (New York: Polish Institute of Arts and Sciences in America, 1960), 114–15.

8. Ibid., 113–14.

9. Ibid, 115.

10. Conrad wrote: "Those who read me know my conviction that the world, the temporal world, rests on a few very simple ideas; so simple that they must be as old as the hills. It rests notably, among others, on the idea of Fidelity." "Conrad on Life and Art," *Heart of Darkness: A Norton Critical Edition,* ed. Robert Kimbrough (New York: Norton, 1988), 218.

11. Meyers, *Joseph Conrad,* 189–90.

12. *The Collected Letters of Joseph Conrad,* ed. Fredereck R. Karl and Laurance Davies (Cambridge: Cambridge University Press, 1986), 2:332.

13. Conrad wrote: "The sea appreciation of one's humble talents has the permanency of the written word, seldom the charm of variety, is formal in its phrasing. There the literary master has the superiority, though he, too, can in effect but say—and often says it in the very phrase—'I highly recommend.' Only usually he uses the word 'We,' there being some occult virtue in the first person plural, which makes it specially fit for critical and royal declarations. I have a small handful of these sea appreciations; signed by various masters, yellowing slowly in my writing-table's left-hand drawer, rustling under my reverent touch, like a handful of dry leaves plucked for a tender memento from the tree of knowledge. Strange! It seems that it is for these few bits of paper, headed by the names of a few ships and signed by the names of a few Scots and English shipmasters, that I

have faced the astonished indignations, the mockeries and the re-
proaches of a sort hard to bear for a boy of fifteen; that I have been
charged with the want of patriotism, the want of sense, and the want
of heart too; that I went through agonies of self-conflict and shed secret tears not a few, and had the beauties of the Furca Pass spoiled
for me, and have been called an 'incorrigible Don Quixote,' in allu-
sion to the book-born madness of the knight. For that spoil! They
rustle, those bits of paper—some dozens of them in all." *A Personal
Record* (London: Thomas Nelson, 1912), 229–30.

14. Naipaul, "Conrad's Darkness and Mine," in *Literary Occasions,*
173.

15. A term used by the Swedish Academy in announcing the 2001
Noble Prize in Literature: "Naipaul is Conrad's heir as the annalist of
the destinies of empires in the moral sense: what they do to human
beings. His authority as a narrator is grounded in his memory of what
others have forgotten, the history of the vanquished."

16. Nabokov, *Strong Opinions,* 42.

17. Joseph Conrad, *Selected Stories* (Ware, Hertfordshire: Words-
worth Classics, 1997), 11.

18. *Notes on Prosody: From the Commentary to His Translation of Pushkin's Eugene Onegin* (New York: Pantheon, 1964). Nabokov was quite
ignorant of English versification when he started writing in English. This is shown in his exchange of letters with Edmund Wilson in
1942. See *Nabokov-Wilson Letters,* ed. Simon Karlinsky (New York:
Harper & Row, 1979), 71–84.

19. A thesis written by Gary Wihl gives an intelligent and com-
prehensive examination of Nabokov's prosodic approach. Wihl also
quoted from Christopher Ricks, the only major book reviewer who
perceived the value of Nabokov's theory: "The 100 page appendix
on prosody animates that corpse of a topic and seems to me to
break important new ground in its definition and English instances."
"Nabokov's Theory of Prosody" (thesis, McGill University, 1978), 1.

20. Nabokov seemed aware that he was not as strong a poet as a
prose writer. In his essay "Reply to My Critics," he wrote, "If told I
am a bad poet, I smile; but if told I am a poor scholar, I reach for my
heaviest dictionary." *The Portable Nabokov,* ed. Page Stegner (New
York: Penguin, 1968), 300.

21. Nabokov, *Poems and Problems* (New York: McGraw-Hill,
1970), 155.

22. Nabokov, *Pnin* (New York: Vintage, 1989), 128.

23. Nabokov, *Strong Opinions,* 106.

24. Ibid, 54.

25. In Conrad's case, he occasionally presents some seamen's rough English vividly, but in general he is weak in dialogue.

26. Stanislaw Baranczak, "Tongue-Tied Eloquence: Notes on Language, Exile, and Writing," in *Altogether Elsewhere: Writers on Exile,* ed. Marc Robinson (Boston and London: Faber, 1994), 250–51.

27. Nabokov protested to his friend Edmund Wilson about this sentence Wilson had added to his essay based on an original review of Nabokov's book *Nikolai Gogol:* "Mr. Nabokov's mastery of English almost rivals Joseph Conrad's." In his letter to Wilson, Nabakov said, "Conrad knew how to handle *readymade* English better than I; but I know better the other kind. He never sinks to the depths of my solecisms, but neither does he scale my verbal peaks." *Nabokov-Wilson Letters,* 253.

28. Nabokov, *Pnin,* 89.

29. *Nabokov-Wilson Letters,* 29.

30. Nabokov, *Pnin,* 16, 33, 156, 157, and 188.

31. Here Nabokov differs from Joyce whose verbal playfulness is not based on misuse but on the fantastic "combination" or "reformation" of words. In *Ulysses,* we come across expressions like "the scrotumtightening sea," "dewsilky cattle," "allwombing tomb," "a rag of wolf's tongue redpanting from his jaw," and "I am almosting it." Those verbal games do not originate from mistakes or distortions, and at most they have stretched grammatical rules.

32. Nabokov, *Strong Opinions,* 184.

33. Nabokov, *Pnin,* 17–18.

34. Ibid, 34.

35. Ibid, 150–51.

36. A student of Nabokov recalled: "Tolstoy was A-plus. Pushkin and Chekhov were A. Turgeneve A-minus. Gogol was B-minus. And Dostoevsky was C-minus. (Or was he D-plus?)." *Vlanimir Nabokov: A Tribute,* ed. Peter Quennell (London: Weindenfeld & Niccolson, 1979), 37.

37. Ibid., 65.

38. Ibid., 38.

39. Chichikov was traveling in a carriage on a raining night. "Meanwhile, the dogs were barking furiously in all sorts of voices:

one, throwing up his head, drew out his barking as carefully as if he'd been God-knows-how highly paid for it; another chopped off his barks hastily, like a sexton; between them, like a mailwagon bell, rang an indefatigable treble, probably a young puppy; and, finally, the whole was topped by a bass, perhaps some patriarch or simply one endowed with a stalwart canine nature, since his voice was rumbling—rumbling like that of the contrabass in a choir when the concert reaches its climax and the tenors, anxious to hit a high note, rise on tiptoe and all strive upward, heads thrown back, while he alone squats down, sinks almost to the very ground, burying his unshaven chin in his collar, and hurls forth his note, making the windowpanes quiver and jar. By the barking alone, produced by such musicians, it was possible to surmise that the village was a sizable one; however, our hero, soaked through and frozen as he was, could think of nothing but bed." Nikolai Gogol, *Dead Souls,* trans. Andrew MacAndrew (New York: Signet, 1961), 52–53. Here, all the magic of presentation is based on the trivial detail of a bunch of barking dogs.

40. David Malouf, *An Imagined Life* (New York: George Braziller, 1978), 98.

41. Amitav Ghosh observes, "But of course the Nobel Prize was itself both symptom and catalyst of a wider condition: the emergence of a notion of a universal 'literature,' a form of artistic expression that embodies differences in place and culture, emotion and aspiration, but in such a way as to render them communicable. This idea may well have had its birth in Europe, but I suspect it met with a much more enthusiastic reception outside." *Incendiary Circumstances* (Boston: Houghton Mifflin, 2005), 108.

42. Salman Rushdie affirms in his essay "Imaginary Homelands": "It is normally supposed that something always gets lost in translation; I cling, obstinately, to the notion that something can also be gained." In *Imaginary Homelands: Essays and Criticism, 1981–1991* (London: Granta Books, 1991), 17.

AN INDIVIDUAL'S HOMELAND

1. C. P. Cavafy, *Collected Poems,* trans. Edmund Keeley and Philip Sherrard (Princeton, N.J.: Princeton University Press, 1992), 36.

2. Later, in Joyce's *Ulysses,* Stephen Dedalus symbolizes Telemachus, Odysseus's son.

3. Belkins Cuza Male, "My Mother's Homeland," trans. Pamela Carmell, in *Looking for Home: Women Writing about Exile,* ed. Deborah Keenan and Roseann Lloyd (Minneapolis: Milkweed Editions, 1990), 154.

4. Homer, *The Odyssey,* trans. E. V. Rieu (Edinburgh: Penguin, 1946), 141–42.

5. Ibid., 213.

6. Ibid., 178–79.

7. *The Inferno of Dante,* trans. Robert Pinsky (New York: Farrar, Straus, 1994), XXVI:107–15.

8. See Mark Musa, *Dante Alligehieri's Divine Comedy,* vol. 2, *Inferno: Commentary* (Bloomington: Indiana University Press, 1996), 350.

9. Quoted in *The Poems of Tennyson,* ed. Christopher Ricks (London: Longman, 1969), 560.

10. Kundera, *Ignorance,* 8.

11. Naipaul, *A Bend in the River,* 20.

12. Hilde Domin, "Heimat," in *Altogether Elsewhere,* 129.

13. W. G. Sebald, *The Emigrants,* trans. Michael Hulese (New York: New Directions, 1997), 182.

14. Quoted in Einar Haugen, *Ole Edvart Rolvaag* (Boston: Twayne Publishers, 1983), 84.

15. O. E. Rolvaag, *Giants in the Earth* (New York: Perennial, 1991), 452.

16. Of course, there had been Indians removed from the land before these European settlers arrived.

Index of Names